THE INTERPENETRATION OF THE UNIVERSES HAS BEGUN.

Paths are opening that will allow us to break out of our circle of limited awareness.

Consciousness is the totality beyond space-time—what may in essence be the real "I." We have come to know that consciousness and energy are one; that all of space-time is constructed by consciousness; that our normal perception of reality is a composite of an indefinite number of universes in which we coexist; and that what we perceive as ourselves is only the localized projection of the totality of our true selves.

Therefore our full energies are devoted to the study of consciousness. There is no other task.

—Bob Toben
From the Foreword of
SPACE-TIME AND BEYOND

BANTAM NEW AGE BOOKS

This important imprint includes books in a variety of fields and disciplines and deals with the search for meaning, growth and change. They are books that circumscribe our times and our future.

Ask your bookseller for the books you have missed.

SPACE-TIME AND BEYOND

TOWARD AN EXPLANATION OF THE UNEXPLAINABLE

THE NEW EDITION

BY BOB TOBEN AND FRED ALAN WOLF
IN CONVERSATION WITH THEORETICAL PHYSICISTS

WITH A NEW SCIENTIFIC COMMENTARY
BY FRED ALAN WOLF

BANTAM BOOKS
TORONTO · NEW YORK · LONDON · SYDNEY · AUCKLAND

IN GRATITUDE TO CARLO SURRÈS
FOR MANY OF THE PROFOUND COSMIC IDEAS
IN THIS BOOK

This low-priced Bantam Book
contains the complete text of the original edition.
NOT ONE WORD HAS BEEN OMITTED.

SPACE-TIME AND BEYOND

A Bantam Book / published by arrangement with
E. P. Dutton, Inc.

PRINTING HISTORY

E. P. Dutton edition published March 1975
6 printings through January 1981
E. P. Dutton (The New Edition) May 1982

New Age and the accompanying figure design as well as the statement
"a search for meaning, growth and change" are trademarks of
Bantam Books, Inc.

Bantam edition / August 1983
2nd printing . . . September 1984
3rd printing . . . May 1987

ISBN 0-553-26656-X

Published simultaneously in the United States and Canada

PRINTED IN THE UNITED STATES OF AMERICA

O   12 11 10 9 8 7 6 5 4

THE NEW EDITION OF 1982

THE DRAWINGS AND NOTES WERE UPDATED
BY BOB TOBEN AND FRED ALAN WOLF

THE NEW SCIENTIFIC COMMENTARY WAS WRITTEN
BY FRED ALAN WOLF

THE EDITOR FOR DUTTON WAS BILL WHITEHEAD

THE ORIGINAL DUTTON EDITION OF 1975

DRAWINGS BY BOB TOBEN
IN CONVERSATION WITH PHYSICISTS
AND, IN THE STRUCTURE OF ENERGY SECTION,
FROM CONVERSATIONS WITH CARLO SUARES
AND OTHERS.

THE EDITOR FOR DUTTON WAS BILL WHITEHEAD

CONTENTS

THE IDEA OF THIS BOOK IS TO RELATE
SOME COMMON IDEAS OF PHILOSOPHIES
THROUGHOUT HISTORY TO THE IDEAS
OF SCIENCE IN OUR TIME ...
TO ATTEMPT TO UNDERSTAND
A LITTLE MORE ABOUT
THE NATURE OF REALITY

THE STRUCTURE
OF
SPACE-TIME

THE THOUGHTS PRESENTED
ARE SUPPORTED BY RECENT
SCIENTIFIC THEORY

ALL ARE REFERENCED TO PAPERS AND
COMMENTARY ... FOR THOSE WHO WISH
TO EXPLORE FURTHER

THE WISDOM OF THOUSANDS OF YEARS
OF MYSTICAL EXPERIENCE IS WALKING
HAND IN HAND WITH THE EMERGING
KNOWLEDGE OF OUR SCIENCES.

IMAGINATION IS EXPANDING

THIS IS A POSSIBLE EXPLANATION <u>NOW</u>,
BUT AS CONSCIOUSNESS CHANGES,
OUR UNIVERSES CHANGE,
AND OTHER INTERPRETATIONS MAY MAKE
MORE SENSE THEN

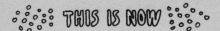 THIS IS NOW

MANY OF THE SCIENTIFIC THEORIES
PRESENTED HEREIN ARE QUITE SPECULATIVE

THE PHYSICAL UNIVERSE DOES <u>NOT</u> EXIST INDEPENDENT OF THE THOUGHT OF THE PARTICIPATORS

POP!

WHAT WE CALL <u>REALITY</u> IS CONSTRUCTED BY THE MIND.

THE WORLD
IS NOT THE SAME
WITHOUT YOU

NOTE:
THESE LITTLE CIRCLES WITH LETTERS IN THEM
REFER TO THE "NEW SCIENTIFIC COMMENTARY"
AT THE BACK OF THIS BOOK.   (A)

WE CONSTRUCT OURSELVES AND WE CONSTRUCT EACH OTHER BEYOND TIME

TIME SEQUENCE HAS NO MEANING, AS THESE CONSTRUCTIONS HAPPEN BEYOND TIME

HOW WE LOOK AT THINGS
AFFECTS WHAT WE LOOK AT
IN VERY SUBTLE WAYS

IN VERY SUBTLE WAYS, HOW WE REGARD OURSELVES
AND OTHERS
CONTINUALLY CHANGES US INTO SOMETHING NEW

AS PERCEIVED FROM WITHIN SPACE-TIME, THESE
UNITS ARE SELF-ORGANIZING

ALL SYSTEMS GO
LIFE PROCESSES FLOW

©

FIELDS ORGANIZE IN A DOUBLE-FLOW PROCESS

QUANTUM WAVE FUNCTIONS
PROVIDE INSTANTANEOUS
RESPONSE TO THE WORLD

QUANTUM WAVES
FORM PATTERNS
IN THE SEA OF LIGHT

©

CAN THOUGHT INFLUENCE
THE STRENGTH OF QUANTUM WAVES ?

DO WE CONSTRUCT THIS REALITY FROM ALL OF TIME ?

ALL WE CAN THINK OR PERCEIVE
IS BROUGHT INTO AWARENESS WITH
OUR INDIVIDUAL THOUGHTS

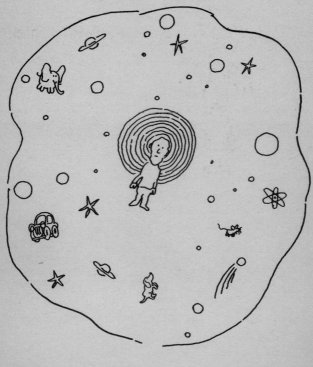

EACH INDIVIDUAL UNIVERSE CONSTRUCTION
ALSO CONTAINS AN INDEFINITE
NUMBER OF <u>OTHER</u> UNIVERSES,
WITH ALL VARIATIONS AND
ALL OTHER POSSIBILITIES

SEE
PAGE
27

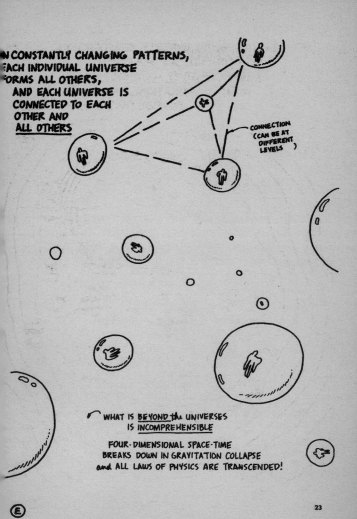

IN CONSTANTLY CHANGING PATTERNS,
EACH INDIVIDUAL UNIVERSE
FORMS ALL OTHERS,
  AND EACH UNIVERSE IS
  CONNECTED TO EACH
  OTHER AND
  ALL OTHERS

CONNECTION
(CAN BE AT
DIFFERENT
LEVELS)

WHAT IS BEYOND the UNIVERSES
    IS INCOMPREHENSIBLE

FOUR-DIMENSIONAL SPACE-TIME
BREAKS DOWN IN GRAVITATION COLLAPSE
and ALL LAWS OF PHYSICS ARE TRANSCENDED!

E

23

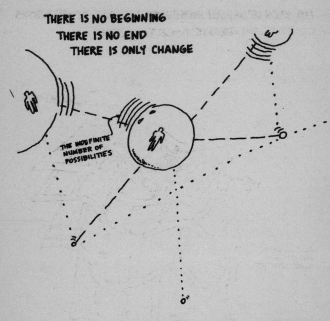

THERE IS NO BEGINNING
THERE IS NO END
THERE IS ONLY CHANGE

THE INDEFINITE
NUMBER OF
POSSIBILITIES

THE CONTINUALLY CHANGING CONNECTIONS
AMONG THE INDIVIDUAL UNIVERSES AND
THE FORMATION OF ALL THE INDIVIDUAL
REALITIES CONSTITUTE A <u>CONTINUAL PROCESS</u>

<u>THERE IS NO BEGINNING AND THERE IS NO END</u>

EACH REALITY
IS CONSTANTLY
FORMING AND
AFFECTING ALL
OTHER REALITIES
BEYOND TIME

FOR EACH OF US, AN INDEFINITE NUMBER OF UNIVERSES EXISTS SIMULTANEOUSLY

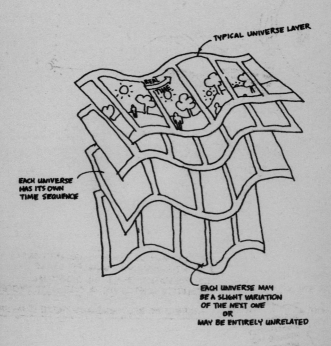

TYPICAL UNIVERSE LAYER

REAL TIME

EACH UNIVERSE HAS ITS OWN TIME SEQUENCE

EACH UNIVERSE MAY BE A SLIGHT VARIATION OF THE NEXT ONE OR MAY BE ENTIRELY UNRELATED

THE "ORDINARY" REALITY WE PERCEIVE IS NOT ONE UNIVERSE

IT IS THE <u>HARMONY</u> OF PHASES OF MOVEMENTS OF AN INDEFINITE NUMBER OF UNIVERSES

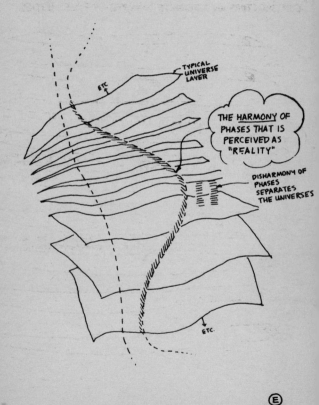

TYPICAL UNIVERSE LAYER

ETC

THE <u>HARMONY</u> OF PHASES THAT IS PERCEIVED AS "REALITY"

DISHARMONY OF PHASES SEPARATES THE UNIVERSES

ETC.

Ⓔ

ALL THINGS ARE POSSIBLE
BUT SOME ARE MORE PROBABLE

THERE IS AN INDEFINITE NUMBER OF HARMONIES
CONSTRUCTING AN INDEFINITE NUMBER OF POSSIBILITIES

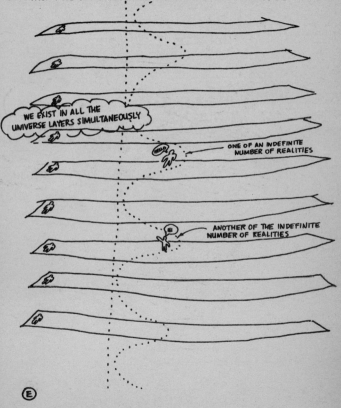

27

A WALL OF LIGHT SEPARATES EACH OF US FROM THE OTHER REALITIES

ALL LIGHT BEAMS COMING FROM
OR GOING TO THE "NOW" MOMENT
MOVE ALONG THE LIGHT CONE

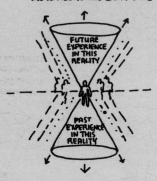

THE WALL OF LIGHT IN 3 DIMENSIONS
IS AN EXPANDING SPHERE OF LIGHT

(F1)

QUANTUM WAVES CAN ACT <u>OUTSIDE</u> THE WALL OF LIGHT

WHEN QUANTUM WAVES ACT
WITHIN THE WALL OF LIGHT,
WE "SEE" ORDINARY EVENTS

QUANTUM WAVES
ACTING OUTSIDE
LIGHT CONES ARE
THE QUANTUM POTENTIAL

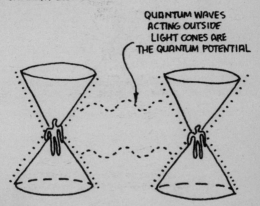

WHEN QUANTUM WAVES ACT OUTSIDE THE WALL OF LIGHT,
WE MAY "FEEL" EVENTS IN WAYS THAT ARE NORMALLY
CONSIDERED TO BE IMPOSSIBLE

THE ONLY WAY TO BREAK THROUGH OUR LIGHT CONES IS WITH THOUGHT

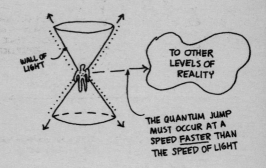

WALL OF LIGHT

TO OTHER LEVELS OF REALITY

THE QUANTUM JUMP MUST OCCUR AT A SPEED <u>FASTER</u> THAN THE SPEED OF LIGHT

GRAVITATION REORGANIZES LIGHT TO
INTERPENETRATE THE UNIVERSES

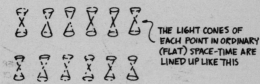

THE LIGHT CONES OF
EACH POINT IN ORDINARY
(FLAT) SPACE-TIME ARE
LINED UP LIKE THIS

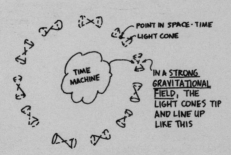

POINT IN SPACE-TIME
LIGHT CONE

TIME
MACHINE

IN A <u>STRONG
GRAVITATIONAL
FIELD</u>, THE
LIGHT CONES TIP
AND LINE UP
LIKE THIS

ONLY IN THIS WAY CAN THEY
JUMP THROUGH THE BLACKHOLE;
CROSS THE SINGULARITY INTO
ANOTHER HARMONY

IT IS POSSIBLE TO TRAVEL IN TIME/SPACE TO THE PAST, THE FUTURE, AND EVEN OTHER UNIVERSES

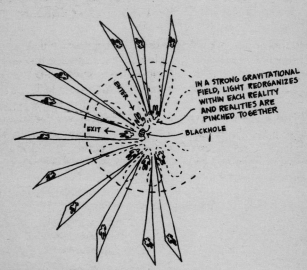

IN A STRONG GRAVITATIONAL FIELD, LIGHT REORGANIZES WITHIN EACH REALITY AND REALITIES ARE PINCHED TOGETHER

ENTER

EXIT ←

BLACKHOLE

TRAVEL OCCURS WHEN THERE IS A JUMP THROUGH THE RING SINGULARITY IN THE INTERIOR OF A ROTATING BLACKHOLE, WHERE THE UNIVERSE LAYERS (HARMONIES) MEET

ALL THINGS ARE INTERCONNECTED

EVERY PART OF YOUR UNIVERSE
IS DIRECTLY CONNECTED TO
EVERY OTHER PART

ANCIENT PROVERB

IF YOU CUT A BLADE
OF GRASS, YOU SHAKE
THE UNIVERSE!

(H)

ALL THINGS ARE INTERCONNECTED IN THE MICROCOSMOS

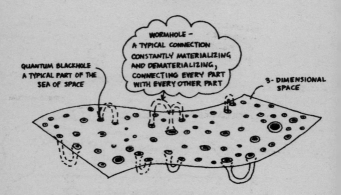

EVERY PART IS DIRECTLY CONNECTED TO EVERY
OTHER PART THROUGH THE WORMHOLES OF SPACE

AT THIS LEVEL OF QUANTUM GRAVITY,
THERE IS NO TIME OR DISTANCE
SEPARATING PARTS

THE DESCRIPTION OF ANY PART IS INSEPARABLE
FROM THE DESCRIPTION OF THE WHOLE

CONNECTIONS CANNOT BE PERCEIVED IN ORDINARY STATES OF CONSCIOUSNESS

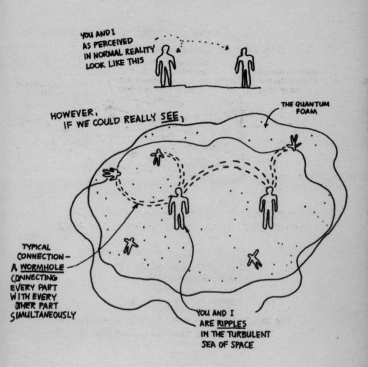

YOU AND I
AS PERCEIVED
IN NORMAL REALITY
LOOK LIKE THIS

HOWEVER,
IF WE COULD REALLY <u>SEE</u>)

THE QUANTUM FOAM

TYPICAL
CONNECTION—
A <u>WORMHOLE</u>
CONNECTING
EVERY PART
WITH EVERY
OTHER PART
SIMULTANEOUSLY

YOU AND I
ARE <u>RIPPLES</u>
IN THE TURBULENT
SEA OF SPACE

YOU CANNOT MOVE WITHOUT INFLUENCING EVERYTHING
IN YOUR UNIVERSE

YOU CANNOT EVEN OBSERVE ANYTHING WITHOUT CHANGING
THE OBJECT AND EVEN YOURSELF

QUANTUM OF ENERGY
FROM AN ENERGY SOURCE
TOUCHES THE OBJECT,
CAUSES THE ATOMS TO
VIBRATE, SUBTLY
CHANGING THE OBJECT.

REFLECTED ENERGY
FROM THE OBJECT
TOUCHES AND CHANGES
THE OBSERVER.

IT IS POSSIBLE THAT JUST <u>THINKING</u> ABOUT AN OBJECT CAN CHANGE IT AND YOURSELF

WHEN
A PARTICIPATOR
THINKS ABOUT
AN OBJECT

THIS CHANGES THE
QUANTUM WAVE FUNCTION
OF THE PARTICIPATOR

WHICH DIRECTLY AFFECTS
THE QUANTUM POTENTIAL

WHICH AFFECTS THE
QUANTUM WAVE FUNCTION
OF THE OBJECT

THE OBJECT SUBTLY CHANGES
AFTER "FEELING" THE
INSTANTANEOUS QUANTUM
FORCE OPERATING OUTSIDE
THE WALL OF LIGHT.

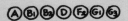

ALL THE UNIVERSE IS ALIVE
ALL THE UNIVERSE IS INTERCONNECTED

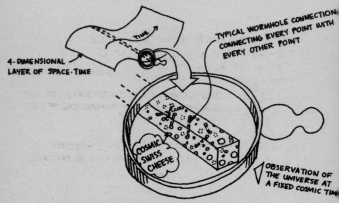

4-DIMENSIONAL LAYER OF SPACE-TIME

TIME

TYPICAL WORMHOLE CONNECTION CONNECTING EVERY POINT WITH EVERY OTHER POINT

COSMIC SWISS CHEESE

OBSERVATION OF THE UNIVERSE AT A FIXED COSMIC TIME

THE MICROSTRUCTURE OF 3-DIMENSIONAL SPACE RESEMBLES A CONSTANTLY <u>FLUCTUATING</u> SWISS CHEESE

INFORMATION TRANSMITS THROUGH THE WORMHOLES AT ORDINARY SPEEDS (WHICH APPEAR TO BE FASTER THAN THE SPEED OF LIGHT FOR OBSERVERS OUTSIDE THE WORMHOLES), CONNECTING ALL POINTS IN SPACE WITH ALL OTHERS IN AN INDEFINITE NUMBER OF POSSIBLE PATTERNS, CONSTANTLY CHANGING, AND TURNING ON AND OFF AT INCREDIBLE FREQUENCIES UP TO 100000000000000000000000000000000000000000000000000000000 TIMES PER SECOND!

38

THE UNIVERSES SELF-ORGANIZE

THE PATTERNS OF THE COSMIC SWISS CHEESE
SELF-ORGANIZE IN A MANNER SIMILAR TO
THAT OF THE HUMAN BRAIN

SELF-ORGANIZATION IS NECESSARY FOR OUR
CURRENT SCIENTIFIC DEFINITION OF LIFE

SO IF EVERYTHING IS MADE OF COSMIC
SWISS CHEESE, EVERYTHING IS PROBABLY
ALIVE

IS THERE LIFE IN EVERYTHING?

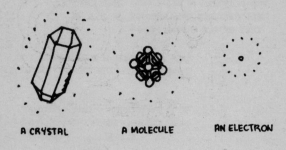

A CRYSTAL   A MOLECULE   AN ELECTRON

AT THE SUBMICROSCOPIC LEVEL,
EVERYTHING IS MOVING, CHANGING,
VIBRATING, GROWING, DISSIPATING

TIME IS NOT ABSOLUTE
SPACE IS NOT ABSOLUTE

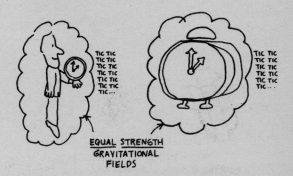

EQUAL STRENGTH
GRAVITATIONAL
FIELDS

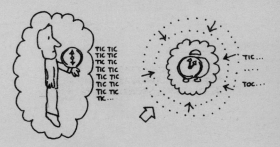

IN A STRONG GRAVITATIONAL FIELD
RELATIVE TO THAT OF THE OBSERVER,
TIME GOES SLOWER AND
DIMENSIONS CONTRACT
FROM THE VIEW OF THE OBSERVER

A CLASSICAL PARTICLE MAY HAVE NO FIXED SIZE BECAUSE GRAVITY CHANGES SPACE AND TIME

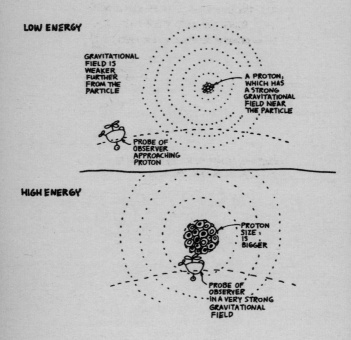

LOW ENERGY

GRAVITATIONAL FIELD IS WEAKER FURTHER FROM THE PARTICLE

A PROTON, WHICH HAS A STRONG GRAVITATIONAL FIELD NEAR THE PARTICLE

PROBE OF OBSERVER APPROACHING PROTON

HIGH ENERGY

PROTON SIZE IS BIGGER

PROBE OF OBSERVER IN A VERY STRONG GRAVITATIONAL FIELD

SPACE IS A CONSTRUCT OF THOUGHT

ALL THE UNIVERSE CAN BE CONTAINED
IN A POINT SMALLER THAN THIS
(TO AN OBSERVER REMAINING AT OUR LEVEL)

AND WE MIGHT STILL EXPERIENCE
SPACE AS WE KNOW IT.

43

THE WHOLE OF THE UNIVERSE, ALL KNOWLEDGE IS CONTAINED WITHIN EACH INDIVIDUAL AND EACH THING

ME TOO!

ME TOO!

ANCIENT PROVERB —
KNOW A GRAIN OF SAND
COMPLETELY AND YOU KNOW
THE UNIVERSE IN ITS ENTIRETY

THIS BECOMES APPARENT IF WE
OBSERVE THE MICROCOSMOS · · · · · · · · · · · · →

EVERY PART CONTAINS THE WHOLE

ONE ELECTRON IS ALL ELECTRONS
ONE PARTICLE IS ALL PARTICLES

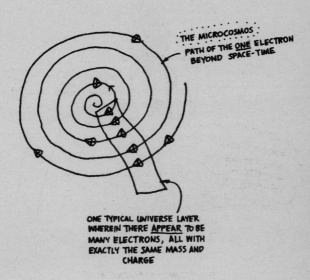

THE MICROCOSMOS
PATH OF THE ONE ELECTRON
BEYOND SPACE-TIME

ONE TYPICAL UNIVERSE LAYER
WHEREIN THERE APPEAR TO BE
MANY ELECTRONS, ALL WITH
EXACTLY THE SAME MASS AND
CHARGE

45

"MATTER" MAY BE NOTHING BUT GRAVITATIONALLY TRAPPED LIGHT (ENERGY)

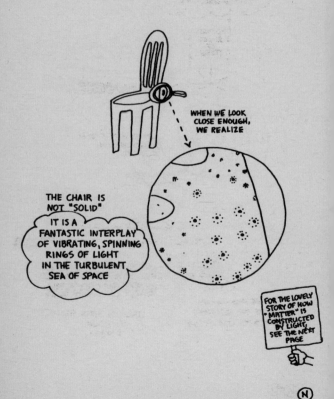

WHEN WE LOOK CLOSE ENOUGH, WE REALIZE

THE CHAIR IS NOT "SOLID"

IT IS A FANTASTIC INTERPLAY OF VIBRATING, SPINNING RINGS OF LIGHT IN THE TURBULENT SEA OF SPACE

FOR THE LOVELY STORY OF HOW "MATTER" IS CONSTRUCTED BY LIGHT, SEE THE NEXT PAGE

IS MATTER GRAVITATIONALLY TRAPPED LIGHT?

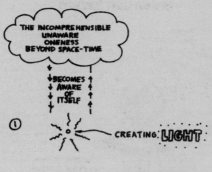

THE INCOMPREHENSIBLE
UNAWARE
ONENESS
BEYOND SPACE-TIME

↓ BECOMES ↑
↓ AWARE ↑
↓ OF ↑
↓ ITSELF ↑

① CREATING LIGHT

② LIGHT CHASES ITSELF
IN GRAVITATIONAL
COLLAPSE!

A VIBRATING
RING OF LIGHT

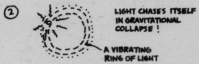

③ FORMING A QUANTUM (MINI) BLACKHOLE

CENTIMETER DIAMETER

THE FUNDAMENTAL
UNIT OF MATTER

AT THE SINGULARITY
INSIDE THE BLACKHOLE
THERE IS NO SPACE OR TIME

COULD BE MADE FROM
QUANTUM
FOAM

NO

47

A CLOSE LOOK AT A ROTATING BLACKHOLE

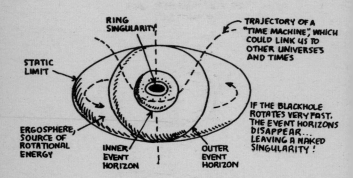

RING SINGULARITY

TRAJECTORY OF A "TIME MACHINE", WHICH COULD LINK US TO OTHER UNIVERSES AND TIMES

STATIC LIMIT

IF THE BLACKHOLE ROTATES VERY FAST, THE EVENT HORIZONS DISAPPEAR... LEAVING A NAKED SINGULARITY!

ERGOSPHERE, SOURCE OF ROTATIONAL ENERGY

INNER EVENT HORIZON

OUTER EVENT HORIZON

A "BUBBLE" IN THE QUANTUM FOAM
COULD LOOK LIKE THIS

BUBBLES IN THE QUANTUM FOAM ARE EVERYWHERE
WE ARE "RIPPLES" IN A SEA OF THEM

THE SIZE OF THE MINI-BLACKHOLE / BUBBLE
IS NOT ABSOLUTE

IT GETS BIGGER IF OBSERVED FROM CLOSE IN

MINI BLACKHOLES MAY BE LIKE
THIS ASTROPHYSICAL BLACKHOLE,
WHICH IS IMMENSELY LARGER

ANTI MATTER IS MATTER IN A REVERSED TIME FLOW

IS THE WHITEHOLE / BLACKHOLE THE FUNDAMENTAL UNIT OF MATTER?

THE SAME PROCESS THAT FORMS BLACKHOLES FORMS WHITEHOLES, ONLY TIME IS REVERSED!

SO TIME IS FLOWING IN TWO DIRECTIONS

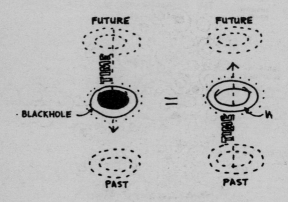

WE ARE NORMALLY ONLY AWARE
OF ITS FLOWING IN ONE DIRECTION
FROM PAST TO FUTURE

SPACE IS NOT NOTHINGNESS

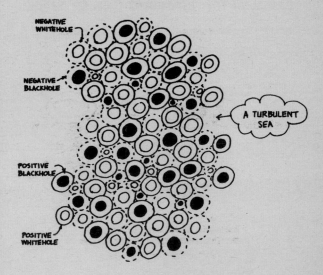

IT IS A TURBULENCE OF CONSTANTLY
APPEARING AND DISAPPEARING (VIRTUAL)
MINI BLACKHOLES AND MINI WHITEHOLES,
BOTH OF EITHER POSITIVE OR NEGATIVE MASS

SUBNUCLEAR PARTICLES ARE MERELY RIPPLES IN THE TURBULENT SEA OF SPACE

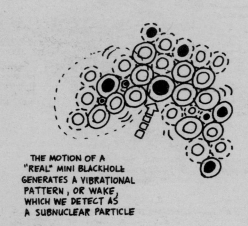

THE MOTION OF A
"REAL" MINI BLACKHOLE
GENERATES A VIBRATIONAL
PATTERN, OR WAKE,
WHICH WE DETECT AS
A SUBNUCLEAR PARTICLE

ATOMS ARE FORMED BY INTERACTIONS BETWEEN VIBRATIONAL PATTERNS

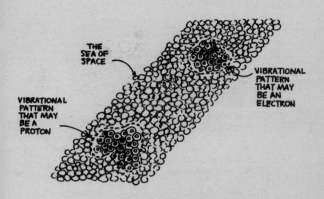

THE
SEA OF
SPACE

VIBRATIONAL
PATTERN
THAT MAY
BE AN
ELECTRON

VIBRATIONAL
PATTERN
THAT MAY
BE A
PROTON

THE ATOMS INTERACT TO FORM MOLECULES,
WHICH INTERACT AND WHICH WE DETECT AS
OUR PHYSICAL "BODIES"

BEYOND SPACE-TIME IS EVERYWHERE

WITHIN EVERY POINT OF OURSELVES

WITHIN EVERY POINT IN SPACE

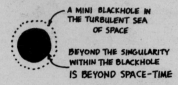

A MINI BLACKHOLE IN
THE TURBULENT SEA
OF SPACE

BEYOND THE SINGULARITY
WITHIN THE BLACKHOLE
IS BEYOND SPACE-TIME

EVERYTHING IS MADE OF WHITEHOLE/BLACKHOLES,
SO (BEYOND SPACE-TIME) IS NOT OUT THERE
IT IS NOT BEYOND THE GALAXIES
IT IS WITHIN EVERYTHING!

Ⓠ

MATHEMATICIANS CAN DESCRIBE THE LIMITS OF SPACE-TIME

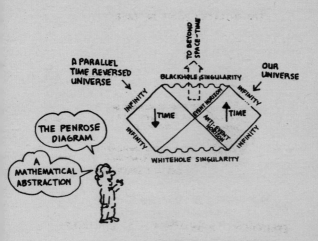

BUT THEY CAN'T DESCRIBE WHAT IS
BEYOND

THEY ONLY KNOW THERE IS A BEYOND

WE ONLY KNOW THAT THERE IS
SOMETHING OTHER THAN SPACE-TIME

BUT WE DON'T KNOW WHAT IT IS!

BECAUSE

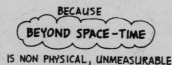

BEYOND SPACE-TIME

IS NON PHYSICAL, UNMEASURABLE

AT THE SINGULARITY ALL LAWS
OF PHYSICS COLLAPSE

BUT WHAT IS BEYOND SPACE-TIME
IS WITHIN EVERYTHING

CAN IT CONNECT WITH US AND INFLUENCE US
WITHIN SPACE-TIME?

IS IT PURE

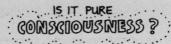

CONSCIOUSNESS?

OR, PERHAPS EVEN BETTER —

PURE AWARENESS

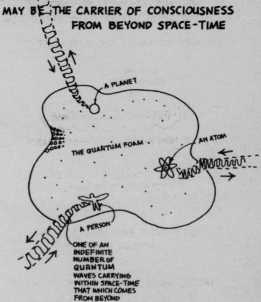

QUANTUM WAVES
MAY BE THE CARRIER OF CONSCIOUSNESS
FROM BEYOND SPACE-TIME

A PLANET

AN ATOM

THE QUANTUM FOAM

A PERSON

ONE OF AN
INDEFINITE
NUMBER OF
QUANTUM
WAVES CARRYING
WITHIN SPACE-TIME
THAT WHICH COMES
FROM BEYOND

THE SCALE OF ORGANIZATION IN SPACE-TIME
IS DETERMINED BY THE WAVE

THE DEGREE OF SELF-ORGANIZATION OF MATTER
IS DETERMINED BY THE RESPONSE
OF THE TURBULENT SEA TO THE WAVE

Ⓠ Ⓒ Ⓓ Ⓙ₁

THE FLOW FROM BEYOND TO WITHIN SPACE-TIME MOVES IN BOTH DIRECTIONS

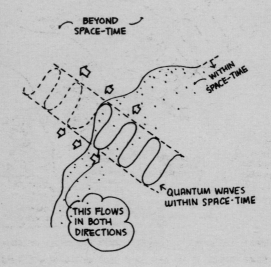

BEYOND
SPACE-TIME

WITHIN
SPACE-TIME

QUANTUM WAVES
WITHIN SPACE-TIME

THIS FLOWS
IN BOTH
DIRECTIONS

DO 'ALL THINGS IN ALL LEVELS OF ORGANIZATION MOVE IN BASIC SYNCHROSIMILARITY?

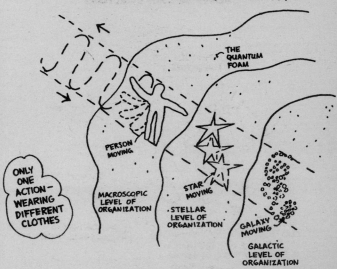

THE QUANTUM FOAM

PERSON MOVING

ONLY ONE ACTION — WEARING DIFFERENT CLOTHES

MACROSCOPIC LEVEL OF ORGANIZATION

STAR MOVING

STELLAR LEVEL OF ORGANIZATION

GALAXY MOVING

GALACTIC LEVEL OF ORGANIZATION

DIFFERENT SIZE WAVES DETERMINE DIFFERENT LEVELS OF ORGANIZATION
BUT SINCE THERE IS NO ABSOLUTE SIZE WITHIN SPACE-TIME,
THE SIZE OF THE WAVE IS DIRECTLY DEPENDENT UPON HOW IT IS OBSERVED

SO WE CAN SPECULATE —

THERE ARE ONLY ARCHETYPAL MOVEMENTS

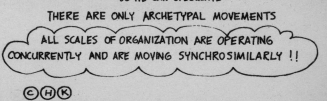

ALL SCALES OF ORGANIZATION ARE OPERATING CONCURRENTLY AND ARE MOVING SYNCHROSIMILARLY !!

© H K

IS GRAVITATION THE MASTER FIELD?

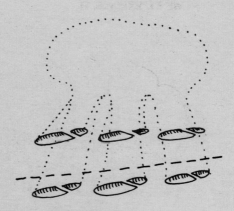

ELECTROMAGNETIC FIELDS
ARE MERELY "FOOTPRINTS"
IN THE CURVATURE OF SPACE

EVEN NUCLEAR FIELDS ARE
JUST HEAVY SHORT RANGE
GRAVITATIONAL FIELDS

THE WEAK FIELDS THAT
MAKE NEUTRINOS ARE
ALSO "FOOTPRINTS" IN
THE CURVATURE OF SPACE

Ⓠ

VIBRATIONS OF THOUGHT PATTERNS
IN SPECIFIC HARMONIES
STRUCTURE ALL "MATTER" AND LIGHT
AS WE EXPERIENCE IT

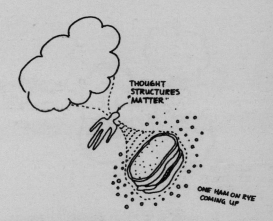

THOUGHT STRUCTURES "MATTER"

ONE HAM ON RYE COMING UP

A HAM ON RYE IS MERELY A RIPPLE, OR FLUCTUATION CONSTRUCTED BY THOUGHT IN THE QUANTUM FOAM OF SPACE

THE MIND MAY BE A REALITY PROCESSOR

ALLOWING ONLY A TINY AWARENESS SO THAT
REALITY CAN BE CONSTRUCTED AND REFINED

ALLOWING US TO FOCUS ON SPECIFIC EVENTS
AND TO EXPERIENCE THE UNIVERSE RICHLY!

?

PARANORMAL
PHENOMENA

?

A POSSIBLE EXPLANATION
FOR SOME EXPERIENCES THAT
BY THEIR NATURE ARE
NEARLY IMPOSSIBLE TO
SCIENTIFICALLY OBSERVE

"UNEXPLAINABLE"
"PSYCHIC," "PARAPSYCHOLOGICAL" PHENOMENA
BOMBARD OUR UNIVERSE

THE "EXPLANATIONS" PRESENTED HERE ARE
DESCRIPTIONS OF THE VISIONARY PHYSICISTS

THESE ARE NOT "THE REASON WHY"

JUST A TEMPORARY VIEW OF THINGS
FROM WITHIN SPACE-TIME

THESE "EXPLANATIONS" WILL CHANGE
AS THE WORLD CHANGES

THE "UNEXPLAINABLE" EVENTS DESCRIBED HEREIN
DEFY CLASSICAL PHYSICS
BUT <u>ARE</u> WITHIN THE REALM OF UNDERSTANDING
OF THE NEW PHYSICS

AN ALTERED STATE OF
CONSCIOUSNESS MAY
BE NECESSARY FOR
THESE EVENTS TO
OCCUR

AT THE "ORDINARY" LEVEL OF CONSCIOUSNESS,
THESE EVENTS CANNOT BE WILLED AND ARE
USUALLY SPONTANEOUS AND UNPREDICTABLE

®₁

?

PSYCHOKINESIS

CAN ENERGY/MATTER FIELDS BE INFLUENCED BY THOUGHT?

MAKE SPACE GLOW WITH LIGHT

RESHAPE LIGHT INTO AN OBJECT

CHANGE TEMPERATURE OF WATER

CAUSE A PHOTO TO APPEAR ON FILM WITHOUT A CAMERA

BEND A SPOON

DEFLECT A LASER BEAM

INFLUENCE AN ELECTROMAGNETIC FIELD

IN ALL CASES, THOUGHT CAN AFFECT THE QUANTUM POTENTIAL,
WHICH MIGHT BE SHAPED TO AFFECT THE ORDINARY FORCES THAT GIVE ENERGY/MATTER ITS IDENTITY AND TO AFFECT GRAVITATIONAL FIELDS ON THE QUANTUM LEVEL

A FEW EXAMPLES FOLLOW

BENDING LIGHT

PSYCHOKINETICALLY

?

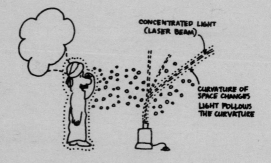

THOUGHT INFLUENCES
THE QUANTUM WAVE,
WHICH MAY INFLUENCE THE
CURVATURE OF SPACE

MATERIALIZATION, DEMATERIALIZATION
PSYCHOKINETICALLY

?

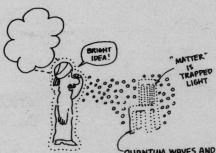

THE LAW OF CONSERVATION
OF ENERGY IS TRANSCENDED,
AS ENERGY CAN BE ABSORBED
OR EMITTED BY SINGULARITIES
OF THE QUANTUM FOAM

QUANTUM WAVES AND GRAVITY
CAN SHAPE "MATTER"
(TRAPPED LIGHT)
FROM LIGHT WITHIN THE
SEA OF SPACE
OR
CAN RETURN MATTER TO
THE SEA OF SPACE

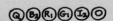

CHANGING WATER TEMPERATURE
PSYCHOKINETICALLY

?

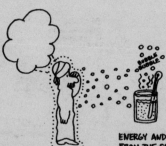

ENERGY AND ENTROPY
FROM THE SINGULARITIES
OF THE QUANTUM FOAM
MAY CAUSE THE WATER
MOLECULES TO JIGGLE
MORE VIOLENTLY,
RAISING THE WATER
TEMPERATURE

THIS PROCESS CAN WORK
IN REVERSE, LOWERING
THE WATER TEMPERATURE

THERE IS NO VIOLATION OF
CONSERVATION OF ENERGY
BECAUSE SINGULARITIES OF
THE QUANTUM FOAM CAN
ABSORB OR EMIT ANY AMOUNT
OF ENERGY

CHANGING METALLIC STRUCTURE
PSYCHOKINETICALLY

?

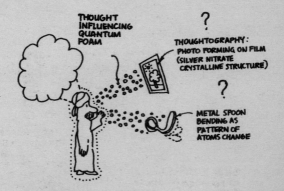

THOUGHT
INFLUENCING
QUANTUM
FOAM

?

THOUGHTOGRAPHY:
PHOTO FORMING ON FILM
(SILVER NITRATE
CRYSTALLINE STRUCTURE)

?

METAL SPOON
BENDING AS
PATTERN OF
ATOMS CHANGE

QUANTUM POTENTIAL CAN
CHANGE THE PATTERN OF
ATOMS WITHIN THE CRYSTALLINE
STRUCTURE OF METAL

TIME TRAVEL
SPACE TRAVEL
ASTRAL TRAVEL

?

IS IT POSSIBLE FOR CONSCIOUSNESS TO ENTER
ANY SPACE-TIME LOCATION — PAST, PRESENT,
OR FUTURE —AND EXPERIENCE THOSE LOCATIONS ?

TRAVEL WITHOUT THE BODY
?

IS IT POSSIBLE TO JUMP AS A
SINGLE POINT OF CONSCIOUSNESS
AND STILL HAVE THE EXPERIENCE! ?

TOTAL KNOWLEDGE OF OTHERS

?

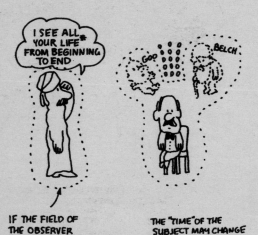

IF THE FIELD OF
THE OBSERVER
CHANGES WITH RESPECT
TO THE SUBJECT,

THE "TIME" OF THE
SUBJECT MAY CHANGE
COMPARED WITH THE
"TIME" OF THE OBSERVER

* PROBABLE LIFE

?

KNOWLEDGE
OF THE

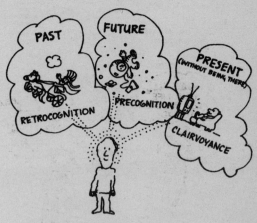

THERE IS NO SUCH THING AS TIME'S DIRECTION
AT THE QUANTUM LEVEL

ALL EVENTS EXIST CONCURRENTLY..
BRIDGES IN THE QUANTUM FOAM
CAN CONNECT ANY EVENT WITH
ANY OTHER EVENT

THOUGHT IS FASTER THAN LIGHT

REINCARNATION

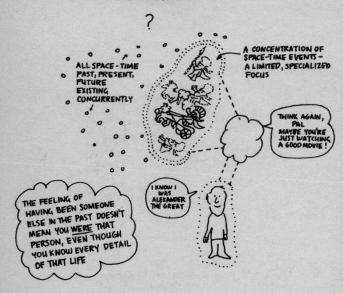

?

ALL SPACE-TIME PAST, PRESENT, FUTURE EXISTING CONCURRENTLY

A CONCENTRATION OF SPACE-TIME EVENTS — A LIMITED, SPECIALIZED FOCUS

THINK AGAIN, PAL MAYBE YOU'RE JUST WATCHING A GOOD MOVIE!

THE FEELING OF HAVING BEEN SOMEONE ELSE IN THE PAST DOESN'T MEAN YOU WERE THAT PERSON, EVEN THOUGH YOU KNOW EVERY DETAIL OF THAT LIFE

I KNOW I WAS ALEXANDER THE GREAT

IF KNOWLEDGE OF THE PAST IS POSSIBLE, IT IS ALSO POSSIBLE TO LINK UP WITH KNOWLEDGE OF AN <u>INTENSE CONCENTRATION OF PAST EVENTS</u> IN SPACE-TIME, INCLUDING EVERY MOMENT OF A LIFETIME OF ANOTHER INDIVIDUAL FROM HISTORY

SO IT IS POSSIBLE TO KNOW THE LIFE DETAILS OF EVERYONE WHO EVER LIVED, NOT ONLY ONE OR TWO SPECIALIZED LIFE PATTERNS!

AURA

?

AURA

A GLOW THAT IS NOT LIGHT,
THAT CANNOT BE PERCEIVED
BY THE NORMAL SENSES,
BUT THAT IS SOMETIMES
SEEN BY PEOPLE IN ALTERED
STATES OF CONSCIOUSNESS

TELEPATHY

?

MESSAGES CAN TRAVEL
INSTANTANEOUSLY
THROUGH WORMHOLES
IN THE SEA OF SPACE

THESE ARE BEYOND SPACE-TIME,
SO DISTANCE IS MEANINGLESS,
AS IS TIME !

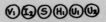

PSYCHOMETRY

?

IS IT POSSIBLE TO OBTAIN THE HISTORY OF AN OBJECT
BY TOUCHING IT ?

DOES THE OBJECT
RETAIN THE
HISTORY OF ALL EVENTS
EXPERIENCED BY
THE OBJECT ?

TELEPORTATION

?

EVERY ACTION IN "REAL" TIME IS AN INDEFINITE
SEQUENCE OF MATERIALIZATIONS AND DEMATERIALIZATIONS
ON THE MICROSCOPIC QUANTUM LEVEL

THEY OCCUR FASTER THAN THE SPEED OF LIGHT
AND IN SUCH GREAT NUMBERS THAT PERCEPTION
OF THIS ACTION IS CONTINUAL

TELEPORTATION COULD RESULT FROM A GIANT QUANTUM JUMP

IMAGINARY
·········>
TIME

LEVITATION
?

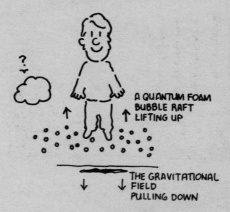

A QUANTUM FOAM
BUBBLE RAFT
LIFTING UP

THE GRAVITATIONAL
FIELD
PULLING DOWN

THE GRAVITATIONAL PULL
COULD DECREASE WHEN
THE QUANTUM FOAM
BUBBLES MEET WITH
THE GRAVITATIONAL
FIELD.

HEALING
WITH THE MIND
?

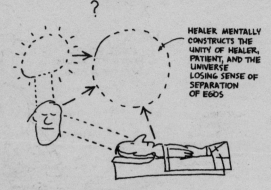

HEALER MENTALLY
CONSTRUCTS THE
UNITY OF HEALER,
PATIENT, AND THE
UNIVERSE
LOSING SENSE OF
SEPARATION
OF EGOS

BECAUSE OF THE INTERCONNECTEDNESS
OF BOHM'S NON LOCAL QUANTUM POTENTIAL,
TIME OR DISTANCE IS IRRELEVANT

<u>THOUGHT</u> CAN UNITE ALL
ALLOWING PHASE HARMONY ENTRAINMENT

ALLOWING THE PATIENT'S BODY TO RE ESTABLISH
ITS NORMAL STATE OF HEALTH

HEALING

WITH THE HANDS

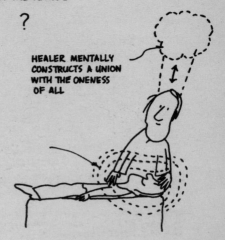

?

HEALER MENTALLY
CONSTRUCTS A UNION
WITH THE ONENESS
OF ALL

TOUCHING,
FORMING A
SOLID BRIDGE
OR CONNECTION
ALLOWING
PHASE HARMONY
ENTRAINMENT

A LINK IS ESTABLISHED BETWEEN THE PATIENT
AND THE HARMONY OF THE UNIVERSE, WHICH
CONTAINS THE KNOWLEDGE, OR "VIBRATIONS,"
TO REESTABLISH A NORMAL STATE OF HEALTH

IT IS POSSIBLE TO BE INFLUENCED BY
HIGHER LEVELS OF CONSCIOUSNESS

INTUITIVE FLASHES
ARE AN EXAMPLE OF
QUANTUM JUMPS
CONNECTING DIFFERENT
STATES OF CONSCIOUSNESS

MICROSCOPIC
QUANTUM WAVES
MERGE INTO GIANT
QUANTUM WAVES

IT IS POSSIBLE TO ALLOW OURSELVES TO BE MORE
RECEPTIVE TO THESE CONNECTIONS TO OTHER LEVELS

-THE MORE THEY CONNECT, THE MORE CONSCIOUSNESS
SPILLS OVER AND STAYS WITH US IN OUR SPACE-TIME
EXISTENCE

THE STRUCTURE
OF
ENERGY

THESE OBSERVATIONS WERE
SYNERGIZED FROM

KNOWLEDGE SHOWN
BY CARLO SUARÈS

VIEWS OF THE
VISIONARY PHYSICISTS

PATHS OF ALL THE
ENLIGHTENED PEOPLE

ANCIENT WISDOMS

AND

THAT WHICH IS BEYOND

IF YOU WANT TO USE THIS OVERVIEW
CHANGE,

SEE YOU ALONG THE WAY...

CONSCIOUSNESS, THE TOTALITY THAT IS EVERYTHING,
REACHES INTO SPACE-TIME, MANIFESTING ITSELF IN
AN INDEFINITE NUMBER OF WAYS AND PERCEPTIONS

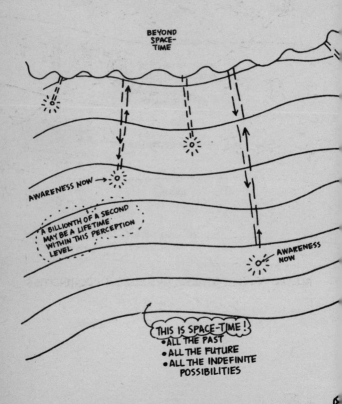

BEYOND
SPACE-
TIME

AWARENESS NOW →

A BILLIONTH OF A SECOND
MAY BE A LIFETIME
WITHIN THIS PERCEPTION
LEVEL

AWARENESS
NOW

THIS IS SPACE-TIME!
• ALL THE PAST
• ALL THE FUTURE
• ALL THE INDEFINITE
  POSSIBILITIES

CONSCIOUSNESS DANCES THROUGH ALL SPACE-TIME

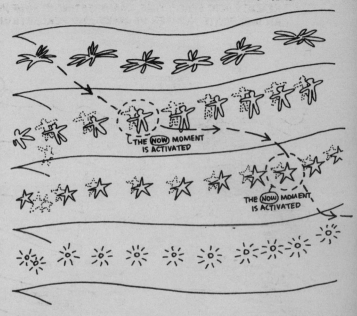

THE (NOW) MOMENT IS ACTIVATED

THE (NOW) MOMENT IS ACTIVATED

ALL THE PASTS, FUTURES, AND ALL THE POSSIBILITIES

THE UNIVERSE IS NOT CONTAINED IN ANYTHING
IT CONTAINS ITSELF

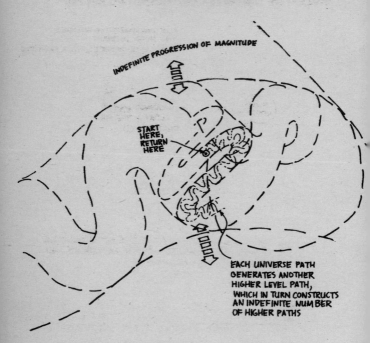

INDEFINITE PROGRESSION OF MAGNITUDE

START HERE, RETURN HERE

EACH UNIVERSE PATH GENERATES ANOTHER HIGHER LEVEL PATH, WHICH IN TURN CONSTRUCTS AN INDEFINITE NUMBER OF HIGHER PATHS

SINCE SPACE AND TIME DO NOT EXIST IN THESE LEVELS, THE "LARGEST" PATH CAN ALWAYS RETURN AND BECOME THE POINT WHERE WE STARTED THE RECOGNITION

WILL EXISTS WITHIN THE CONFINES OF OUR
SPACE-TIME CONTINUUM AND DOES NOT GO BEYOND

WANTING SOMETHING CHANGES
THE THING YOU WANT
— ESSENCE OF THE QUANTUM PRINCIPLE

YOU CANNOT **WANT**
TO FLOAT IN THE AIR
AND SUCCEED

BUT
YOU CAN **LOVE** THE ACT OF FLOATING
AND BE AWARE OF THE BEAUTY AND
HARMONY OF IT

AND MAYBE SOMEDAY THE UNIVERSE
LAYER IN WHICH YOU ARE FLOATING
WILL LINK WITH YOUR PERCEPTION

WE INFLUENCE OUR FUTURES (AND PASTS) DIRECTLY WITH THOUGHT

EVERYTIME YOU <u>THINK</u> OF BEING HAPPY AND HEALTHY, YOU ARE ACTUALLY HAPPY AND HEALTHY IN SOME UNIVERSE LAYER

EVERYTIME YOU <u>THINK</u> OF BEING SICK OR DYING, YOU ACTUALLY ARE SICK OR DYING IN SOME UNIVERSE LAYER

IF YOU <u>THINK</u> ENOUGH UNIVERSE LAYERS, THEY EVENTUALLY COME INTO HARMONY, AND YOUR THOUGHTS BECOME <u>REALITY</u>

THIS IS NOT WILL, IT IS AWARENESS !

EVERY THOUGHT, EVERY DREAM IS AN AWARENESS OF ANOTHER REALITY WHICH COEXISTS

THIS "THOUGHT"
IS ACTUALLY IN
ANOTHER UNIVERSE
LAYER

THIS BOY IS <u>ACTUALLY</u>
<u>FLYING</u> TO THE MOON
IN ANOTHER UNIVERSE LAYER !

THE DIRECT EXPERIENCE WOULD COME WITH A HARMONY
AMONG THE LAYERS

INDIVIDUAL AWARENESS CAN BE GUIDED TO THE MOST HARMONIOUS OF FUTURES

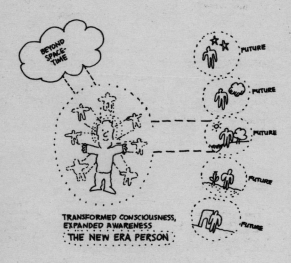

AS ALL FUTURES AND PASTS EXIST CONCURRENTLY

OUR VIEW OF "I" IS EXPANDING

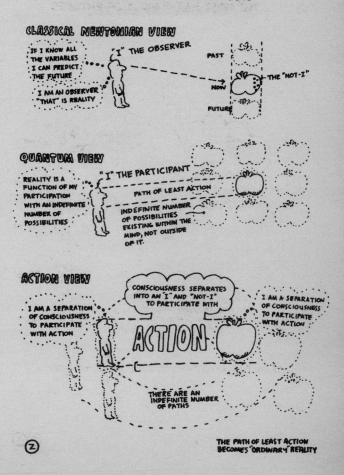

CLASSICAL NEWTONIAN VIEW

IF I KNOW ALL THE VARIABLES I CAN PREDICT THE FUTURE

I AM AN OBSERVER "THAT" IS REALITY

"I" THE OBSERVER

PAST

NOW

FUTURE

THE "NOT-I"

QUANTUM VIEW

REALITY IS A FUNCTION OF MY PARTICIPATION WITH AN INDEFINITE NUMBER OF POSSIBILITIES

"I" THE PARTICIPANT

PATH OF LEAST ACTION

INDEFINITE NUMBER OF POSSIBILITIES EXISTING WITHIN THE MIND, NOT OUTSIDE OF IT.

ACTION VIEW

CONSCIOUSNESS SEPARATES INTO AN "I" AND "NOT-I" TO PARTICIPATE WITH

I AM A SEPARATION OF CONSCIOUSNESS TO PARTICIPATE WITH ACTION

I AM A SEPARATION OF CONSCIOUSNESS TO PARTICIPATE WITH ACTION

ACTION

THERE ARE AN INDEFINITE NUMBER OF PATHS

②

THE PATH OF LEAST ACTION BECOMES 'ORDINARY' REALITY

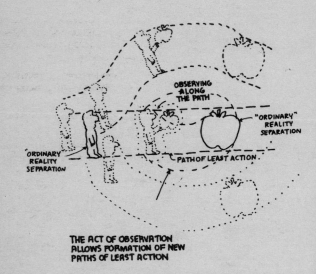

THE ACT OF OBSERVATION
ALLOWS FORMATION OF NEW
PATHS OF LEAST ACTION

CHANGING THE I / NOT-I AWARENESS
CAN CHANGE ORDINARY REALITY

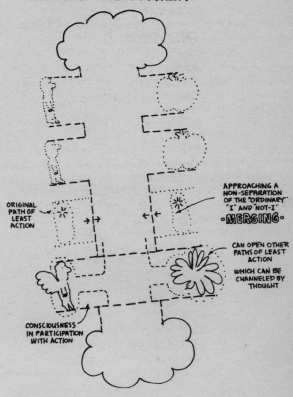

ORIGINAL
PATH OF
LEAST
ACTION

APPROACHING A
NON-SEPARATION
OF THE "ORDINARY"
"I" AND "NOT-I"
-MERGING-

CAN OPEN OTHER
PATHS OF LEAST
ACTION

WHICH CAN BE
CHANNELED BY
THOUGHT

CONSCIOUSNESS
IN PARTICIPATION
WITH ACTION

BASIC ENERGY RELATIONS MANIFEST CONCURRENTLY THROUGHOUT AN INDEFINITE NUMBER OF LEVELS OF PERCEPTION

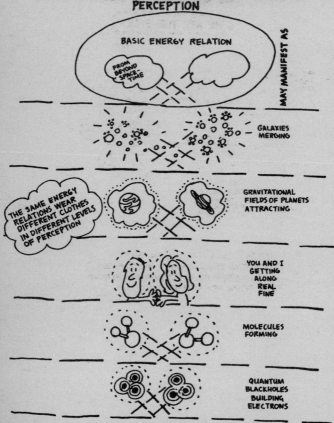

WE JUST EXPERIENCE THE RELATION DIFFERENTLY AT DIFFERENT LEVELS

WE ARE INFLUENCED BY THE STARS
WE INFLUENCE THE STARS
WE ARE THE STARS

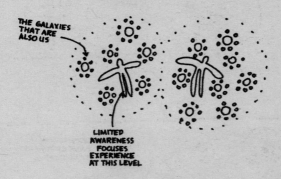

THE GALAXIES THAT ARE ALSO US

LIMITED AWARENESS FOCUSES EXPERIENCE AT THIS LEVEL

WITH A CHANGE IN CONSCIOUSNESS
WE COULD BECOME AWARE OF OURSELVES
AS GALAXIES OR AS OTHER PARTICIPATIONS
AT OTHER PERCEPTION LEVELS

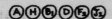

ARE THE PATTERNS IN THE BRAIN THE SAME AS THOSE OF THE UNIVERSE?

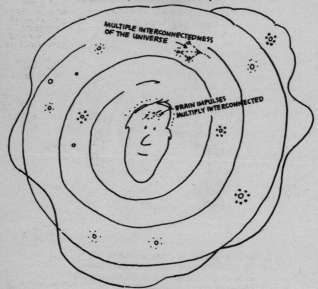

ALL THE UNIVERSE
ALL THE MICROCOSMOS
THE BRAIN

ACT SIMILARLY
CONSTANTLY SWITCHING ON AND OFF
IN MULTIPLE INTERCONNECTEDNESS

WHEN WE GAZE AT THE UNIVERSE, DO WE GAZE AT OUR OWN MINDS?

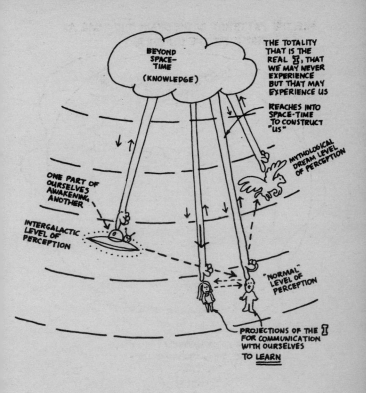

BEYOND SPACE-TIME

(KNOWLEDGE)

THE TOTALITY THAT IS THE REAL I, THAT WE MAY NEVER EXPERIENCE BUT THAT MAY EXPERIENCE US

REACHES INTO SPACE-TIME TO CONSTRUCT "US"

MYTHOLOGICAL DREAM LEVEL OF PERCEPTION

ONE PART OF OURSELVES AWAKENING ANOTHER

INTERGALACTIC LEVEL OF PERCEPTION

"NORMAL" LEVEL OF PERCEPTION

PROJECTIONS OF THE I FOR COMMUNICATION WITH OURSELVES TO LEARN

COMMUNICATION WITH OTHERS IS US TALKING TO OURSELVES SO THAT KNOWLEDGE CAN REEMERGE

AS THE UNIVERSES INTERPENETRATE, KNOWLEDGE CAN COME IN MANY FORMS

SO IF WE HEAR FROM

A SPACEMAN

A BURNING BUSH

OR

THE HEAVENS THEMSELVES

THEY MAY BE PROJECTIONS OF THE REAL US, "REAL" ILLUSIONS THAT ARE RELATED TO OUR EXPERIENCE SO THAT WE CAN ACCEPT THEM AND <u>LEARN</u>

THESE PROJECTIONS <u>ARE</u> REALITIES — EQUALLY AS "REAL"AS THE ILLUSION WE <u>SHARE</u> OF OURSELVES BEING "REAL"

**REINCARNATION FROM THE PAST OR FROM THE FUTURE
ARE ALSO "OURSELVES" TALKING TO "OURSELVES"**

LOCALIZING OR FOCUSING ON
AN ABSTRACTION — A "REAL" ILLUSION
SO THAT WE MAY LEARN

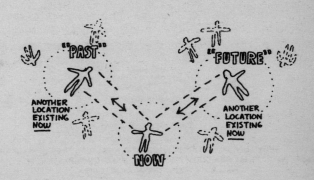

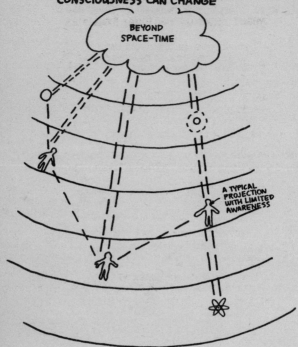

MORE AWARENESS CAN COME
CONSCIOUSNESS CAN CHANGE

BEYOND
SPACE-TIME

A TYPICAL
PROJECTION
WITH LIMITED
AWARENESS

AS WE UNDERSTAND WHAT WE ARE NOT,
WE BECOME AWARE OF THE INDEFINITE
NUMBER OF OURSELVES CO EXISTING
CONCURRENTLY THROUGHOUT "TIME"

INDIVIDUALS WHO MAKE THINGS FLY, BEND, DISAPPEAR OR WHATEVER

MIGHT SHOW US PERSONAL REALITIES

PERHAPS GIVE US MOMENTARY AWARENESS NECESSARY TO CRUMBLE EXISTING ARCHAIC BELIEF SYSTEMS

SCIENTIFIC EXPERIMENTS MAY NOT BE ABLE TO SHOW THIS

INSTRUMENTS AND OBSERVERS CAN CONNECT WITH OTHER "ILLUSIONS"

WE DON'T HAVE TO LEARN HOW TO CONTROL OR DIRECT ENERGIES

AS A MATTER OF FACT, THAT'S KINDA DANGEROUS

{ WE CAN'T EVEN CONTROL
A BOW AND ARROW }

ENERGY TO MOVE OBJECT

ALL WE HAVE TO DO IS ALLOW CONSCIOUSNESS TO FIND US

AND WE CAN LINK UP WITH THAT
HARMONY WHEREIN THE TABLE
IS <u>MOVED</u>

NOTHIN'
TO
IT !

IT'S JUST A
THOUGHT

Ⓔ Ⓧ Ⓦ Ⓨ

THE WAY OF THE NEW ERA

UNDERSTAND ARCHETYPAL ACTIONS

THINK OF AN EVENT THAT IS IN HARMONY
WITH ARCHETYPAL ACTIONS / NATURE

NEW PATHS OF LEAST ACTION CAN DEVELOP
AND BUILD — GUIDING YOUR AWARENESS
TO THAT HARMONY

AND THOUGHT BECOMES EXPERIENCE!

Ⓩ

THERE IS NO DEATH

ONLY A CHANGE OF AWARENESS, A CHANGE OF COSMIC ADDRESS

THE REAL "I" IS BEYOND SPACE-TIME

THERE IS ONLY CHANGE

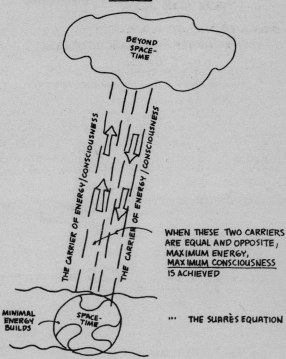

BEYOND SPACE-TIME

THE CARRIER OF ENERGY/CONSCIOUSNESS

THE CARRIER OF ENERGY/CONSCIOUSNESS

WHEN THESE TWO CARRIERS
ARE EQUAL AND OPPOSITE,
MAXIMUM ENERGY,
MAXIMUM CONSCIOUSNESS
IS ACHIEVED

SPACE-TIME

MINIMAL
ENERGY
BUILDS

... THE SUARÈS EQUATION

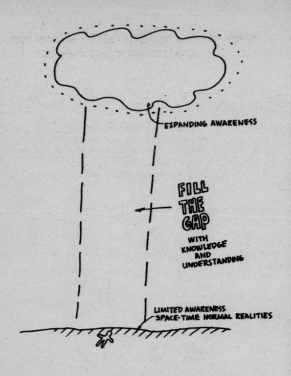

EXPANDING AWARENESS

FILL
THE
GAP

WITH
KNOWLEDGE
AND
UNDERSTANDING

LIMITED AWARENESS
SPACE-TIME NORMAL REALITIES

WE MUST UNDERSTAND THE BASICS

A CHANGE IN CONSCIOUSNESS IS <u>LOST</u> WITHOUT A REAL UNDERSTANDING

WITH UNDERSTANDING
THE DIRECTION OF AWARENESS CAN BE INFLUENCED

WHEN THOUGHT AND EXPERIENCE BECOME ONE, CONSCIOUSNESS HAS CHANGED

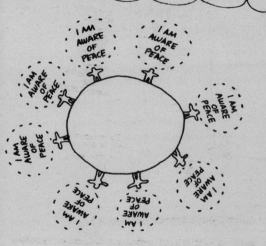

IF ENOUGH PEOPLE (PROJECTIONS OF OURSELVES) ARE AWARE OF THE HARMONIES OF PEACE IN THE UNIVERSE LAYERS, <u>CONFLICT AND FEAR CAN DIMINISH</u>

I AM AWARE OF PEACE

ALL IS CONSTRUCTED FROM THOUGHT

THIS WAS THE SIGNIFICANCE

OF

JESUS !

BUDDHA !

AND

THE HANDFUL OF OTHERS
THROUGHOUT HISTORY

TO SHOW
THE INTERPENETRATION OF THE UNIVERSES

TO REUNITE
OURSELVES WITH OURSELVES

SO NOW —

WITH INCREDIBLE ENERGY
LOCKED INTO SPACE-TIME

IT MAY TAKE 1,000? OR 10,000?
"AWARE" INDIVIDUALS

TO RELEASE THAT ENERGY TOWARD
A TRANSFORMATION OF CONSCIOUSNESS

AS WE TURN INWARD

WE
REALIZE

I
DIRECTLY
AFFECT
THE
UNIVERSES

I TAKE
DIRECT
RESPONSIBILITY

DON'T WAIT FOR THE GURU
DON'T WAIT FOR THE MESSIAH
DON'T WAIT FOR THE SECOND COMING.

THE REAL "I" IS HERE NOW – WITHIN.

WAKE UP AND SMELL THE COFFEE.

SO WHY ARE WE HERE AT ALL ?

SPACE-TIME IS HERE
JUST TO HAVE SOMETHING TO DO

SO WE PLAY
THE GAME

WE DANCE
THE DANCE

THE JOY IS IN THE <u>CHANGE</u>

THE <u>PROCESS</u>

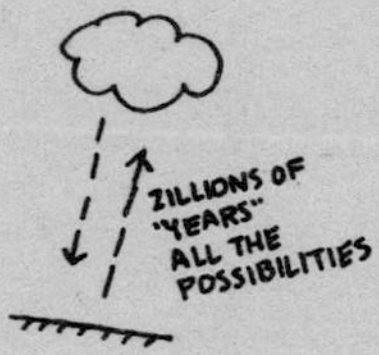

ZILLIONS OF
"YEARS"
ALL THE
POSSIBILITIES

NOT THE ATTAINMENT

WE MAY NEVER COMPLETELY EXPERIENCE
BEYOND SPACE-TIME

YET WE DANCE TOWARD IT

WHAT NOW?

YOU CANNOT BE AWARE OF
WHAT IS BEYOND SPACE-TIME

BUT

YOU CAN WALK IN THIS DREAM
IN CONTACT
WITH THE HIGHER CONSCIOUSNESS
THAT IS THE REAL
YOU

IT WILL FIND YOU

REALIZE
EVERY EVENT IN THE INDEFINITE
NUMBER OF UNIVERSES IS
INFLUENCED BY YOU

REALIZE
THERE IS LIFE IN
EVERYTHING

REALIZE
YOU ARE NOT
WHAT YOU'VE BEEN
TAUGHT

ALLOW
CONSCIOUSNESS
TO UNITE
WITH YOU

AND SOMEDAY

WE WON'T STOP SMILING
. . . .
WHEN WE WALK, WE'LL FLOAT
. . . .
AND LIGHT WILL POUR FROM OUR EYES
. . . .

THE INTERPENETRATION OF THE UNIVERSES HAS BEGUN

NEW SCIENTIFIC COMMENTARY

BY

FRED ALAN WOLF

INTRODUCTORY REMARKS

The following commentary is my attempt to bridge the gap between the facts of modern physics and the understanding of these facts, from the viewpoint both of the scientist and of the general reader. As you can see, these facts lead to controversial interpretations. Much of this controversy is still to be resolved. Do time machines exist? Can we move near to the speed of light? Do I know that matter is nothing more than trapped light? I will answer and comment upon these questions and many others that you may raise to the best of my imaginative ability, and frankly, with a bent toward the mystical, insightful side of human nature. In other words, these are not the answers of a conservative physicist; in all modesty, they are the answers of a visionary physicist. In fact, this whole book can be considered to be visionary physics. Thus, these ideas are to be taken lightly.

What is visionary physics? It is an art form based upon scientific fact and extrapolation from fact into areas of human thought and endeavor that would not normally be included in physics. Visionary physics is the kind of physics done by physicists on the back of envelopes over a cup of coffee. It is "shoptalk" on concepts. It is always a risky business (if taken seriously) and it *must* be speculative to be any good. In other words it should open the doors to new insights, if it is to serve any purpose at all. I hope that this book will open such doors for its readers and encourage them to be more curious about modern physics. I also hope that it will help to communicate to a wider audience how truly magical the physical universe is!

Finally I would like to comment on the overall theme of this book. It was a contention at the time of the writing that the universe and all things in it, including ourselves and our minds, could be explained by combining spiritual thought, quantum physics and Einstein's general theory of relativity. It was in the exciting hope of unifying these realms of modern physics together with spiritual and psychic thought that this commentary was written.

FRED ALAN WOLF
La Jolla, California

Einstein's theory of relativity has shown that space and time are not absolute, as originally thought. Similarly, truth in science is not absolute. All the scientist can do is make models that attempt to describe, predict, and explain experience. Science is simply a magical set of rules and attitudes that works in a certain limited context of experience.

> The basic texture of research consists of dreams into which the threads of reasoning, measurement and calculation are woven.
>
> ALBERT SZENT-GYORGYI

> What quantities are observable should not be our choice, but should be given, should be indicated to us by the theory.

> As far as the laws of mathematics refer to reality, they are not certain; and so far as they are certain, they do not refer to reality.

> Imagination is more important than knowledge.
>
> ALBERT EINSTEIN

> What we need is imagination. We have to find a new view of the world.
>
> RICHARD P. FEYNMAN

> For any speculation which does not at first glance look crazy, there is no hope.
>
> FREEMAN DYSON

Until the discoveries of modern quantum theory in this century, the physical universe and our thoughts about the physical universe were thought to be totally separate. Quantum physics shows us that what we visualize is what we see. In other words, our thoughts about the world and the way the world appears are fundamentally related. The relationship between thought and "reality" is, however, a subtle one. The chair in the drawing on p. 16 is not just made up of little tiny ball-like atoms all jingling around. There are no atoms present until we actually begin to look for them. How is this possible? Well, first of all, atoms have no well-defined boundaries. These fuzzy little things only begin to appear with boundaries when we perform sophisticated experiments which actually destroy the chair.

We have come to learn through quantum physics that no objects have well-defined boundaries. If we can imagine the chair existing without us, just for a moment, its boundaries would become fuzzy too! Its fuzziness would not become apparent, however, for a very long time. It would take over 10 billion years for the chair to fuzz out. But an atom, that's a horse of a different color. Because it is so tiny, it takes only one billionth part of a billionth part of a second for the atom to spread out into fuzziness. And it continues to spread out until you come along and observe it. At that instant, depending on which experiment you perform, the atom is reduced to size.* Just think, without you all atoms would spread out into the universe at an alarming rate. By not looking too closely for atoms, you have given them permission to fuzz their boundaries sufficiently to make up a chair. That's why I say there are no atoms until you choose to look for them. And that is why we say that there is no physical universe without our thoughts about it. Without your observations and thoughts that that object is a chair, it too would fuzz out into oblivion. But don't worry, ten billion years is too long to wait.

Another way to talk about this fuzziness is to call it the principle of uncertainty. Put simply, it says that you cannot know both the position and the path of a moving object. If you determine one of these attributes with perfect accuracy, it will always be at the expense of the other. Thus, even though you make as good an observation as possible, the world is always a little uncertain.

This choice of experiments is called complementarity in physics. It means that there are two complementary ways of determining the behavior of an atom: it can behave like a particle or it can behave like a wave.

By the word "construct" (see p. 17), we mean something special and a little different than you might mean. We mean that what we think of ourselves and of each other determines how we appear to each other and to ourselves. Now this scheme doesn't work instantly; it takes time. The way you are and the way I am has been constructed by long and painstaking thought. I would say that the way I am is the concretization of thought. By changing my thoughts about myself and you, I will change myself and you! But you have more to say about yourself than I do. The way this works is called complementarity. There are always two complementary ways to "construct" reality. If you look at reality one way, the other way becomes undefined. For an atom we say there is a wave-particle complementarity. When the atom appears as a wave (always with other atoms), it never appears as a particle; and when it shows itself as a particle, no wavelike behavior is seen (regardless of how many atoms we look at). When you and a close friend are getting along just fine, there is no clear separation between the two of you; you even notice that you have the same thoughts at the same time! But when you are not getting along so well, you notice your separateness, how different you are from your friend. That's complementarity acting on the human level. As far as we know, every bit of matter or energy exhibits this paradoxical and complementary way of existing. No wonder then that no matter how bad it can be for us one day, the next may be perfect. The universe is a paradox.

The reason that time sequences have no meaning is that this construction procedure (see B₁) begins before matter materializes. The quantum physicist calls the "pre-matter" phase, the quantum wave function. The quantum wave function is very well calculated, but it is not matter! It is not anything, really. Quantum waves can move, and they do so very, very quickly, in fact they can move faster than light. And that means they can go backward or forward in time. Physicists call *things* that can travel faster than light (if there actually are such things), tachyons, which means "things that go fast." Einstein and his followers have shown that anything that moves faster than light can be observed in contrary time sequences. Some observers would see these sequences as a movie, while others would see them as a movie running backward. As fantastic as it sounds, the mathematical models for such things are very well defined and, mathematically at least, well understood. (See reference in note S.)

Another essential property is that the quantum wave represents where and when something is *likely* to occur; in other words, it is a measure of the probability of an event taking place. The exciting idea about this is that this probability not only exists in our minds, but also moves in space and time. In other words this wave is both in our minds *and* out there in the world. The quantum wave, in summary, is a wave of probability moving faster than light and connecting our minds to the physical world.

How does the universe do it? How does it produce anything at all? No one really knows the answer. However, we do know that self-reference is an important part of the process. The way that it works in quantum physics, which underlies all of the physical world, is that the quantum wave (see note B_2) flows between two events just like a river leaving a source and flowing to a sink. But then it "turns around" in space-time and flows back from the sink to the source. The resulting reinforcement between the quantum wave and its space-time reflected image produces the experiences we call reality. In the language of quantum physics, we say that the wave is multiplied by its "complex-conjugated self" to produce the probabilities of the real world. This double-flow process occurs in every physical phenomenon. It is in this manner that we have self-organization; self exists through the wave interacting with its space-time mirrored image in the same way that you interact with your own mirror image. Did you ever notice that in order to notice yourself in a mirror you have to forget yourself? And to forget yourself you have to take note of yourself? By self-reflection we are able to change ourselves. By observing ourselves in others we are able to change each other. All there is, is the one-verse, the universe looking at itself in itself.

I think that thought does modify the strength of quantum wave functions (see B_2). Now, the strength of a quantum wave is a measure of the probability of an event occurring. I believe that the greater the awareness or consciousness of the observer, the greater the probability of the event occurring. Eugene Wigner was one of the first physicists to point out that consciousness modifies the quantum wave and thereby changes the physical universe. This Nobel Laureate wrote in 1967:

> The being with a consciousness must have a different role in quantum mechanics than the inanimate measuring device. . . . In other words, the impression which one gains at an interaction, called also the *result of an observation*, modifies the wave function of the system. The modified wave function is, furthermore, in general unpredictable before the impression gained at the interaction has entered our consciousness: it is the entering of an impression into our consciousness which alters the wave function because it modifies our appraisal of the probabilities for different impressions which we expect to receive in the future. It is at this point that the consciousness enters the theory unavoidably and unalterably.

> Physico-chemical conditions and properties . . . not only create the consciousness, they also influence [the being's] sensations most profoundly. Does, conversely, the consciousness influence the physico-chemical conditions?

In other words, does the human body deviate from the laws of physics, as gleaned from the study of inanimate nature? The traditional answer to this question is "No": the body influences the mind but the mind does not influence the body.

The recognition that physical objects and spiritual values have a very similar kind of reality has contributed in some measure to my mental peace— . . . at any rate, it is the only known point of view which is consistent with quantum mechanics.

E. WIGNER *Symmetries and Reflections*
(Indiana University Press, Bloomington, 1967), pp. 183, 188, 192.

One of the most exciting ideas to come out of quantum physics is the Everett thesis of parallel universes (see reference to DeWitt and Graham). In his Ph.D. thesis Everett decided to take the quantum wave (see B_2) not as an indicator of the probability of something occurring, but as an indicator of what is actually occuring. The reason this is so mind-boggling is that the wave represents the flow in space-time of *all possible events*—even if those events are contradictory to each other! For example, when you flip a coin in the air, it lands on the ground with heads or tails showing, never both sides at the same time. But the coin's quantum wave always gives equal probability of heads or tails showing. How can the wave represent reality? Everett and his followers came up with the answer that for each possibility there exists a parallel universe where the event actually occurs. Thus, in one universe the coin lands heads and in another it lands tails. And even more surprising, you are in both universes observing the coin's fate! You exist in each world.*

*Yet each world is essentially unknown to the other. Thus, each edition of you is aware only of his or her own world. If both editions are taken together, then all possible results from a given interaction actually take place! Each result occurs in a different

But do these separate worlds ever interact? Indeed they do. It is their interaction, or better said, their superposition which creates new possibilities. In other words, by adding together different wave branches, where each wave branch is its own universe, we can produce a new universe. By adding together, so to speak, the heads-wave and the tails-wave, we produce a coin standing on its edge. It is these superpositions which make the process ever-changing and ever-new.

One of the most exciting ideas that came from Einstein's theory of relativity was not due to Einstein himself, but to Hermann Minkowski. It was Minkowski who visualized Einstein's ideas and saw space-time as a picture (see reference to Einstein, Lorentz, Weyl and Minkowski). The picture he drew was called the light cone. It shows a single event occurring at a single point in space and time. From that event, if we move our eyes up the page, we are witnessing the future consequences of that event. If we move our eyes down the page, we are looking at all of the past events that could have influenced the event in question. Similarly, if we move our eyes sideways along the page, we are witnessing events that are all taking place at the same time, but at different points in space. The two cones that extend from the event trace out the boundaries of all past events that could have signaled the event in question, and all future events that could be signaled by the event in question, by a signal that travels at the speed of light or less. All other events are beyond normal, slower-than-light communication with the event in question and are called the elsewhere. Between the inside of the light cone and the elsewhere, we say there is a wall of light, just as there is a wall of sound for an airplane approaching the speed of sound. We use this analogy because no thing

---

world, however. Thus even though the total picture is well behaved and determined, each individual world appears indeterminate.

can travel faster than the speed of light according to relativity. Thus for all matter there is a wall of light.

If consciousness can change quantum wave functions (see D), then thought can leap the walls of light enclosing us. The reason is that quantum waves (see B_2) travel faster than light. A quantum jump is the movement of a thing from one place to another without going in-between. It occurs just like the "Star-Trek" transporter effect. The thing just dissolves in the original spot and appears instantly at another spot. What happens is simply that the wave has undergone a faster-than-light movement of a special kind. We call it a collapse of the wave function, or if you prefer my description, a wave pop. Whenever there is a wave pop, there is a quantum jump. Whenever a quantum jump occurs, our consciousness also undergoes a quantum jump. We become aware of the new position of the thing at the instant the jump occurs. This is what we mean by sudden intuition or sudden knowing. It can't happen without changing the universe at the same time. The connection between knowing an event and the event itself is very, very intimate. This intimacy is much like watching yourself in a mirror. Your image is the thing being observed, and of course you are the observer. Change your awareness of your image and you change your image, don't you?

The idea of a "potential" may be unfamiliar to our readers. Physicists discovered a remarkable principle around the time that Newton was doing his thing. It is called the principle of conservation of energy. It means that whatever process is going on, the *total* energy involved remains the same. This does not mean that energy doesn't change, however; it does, and one of the ways it changes is from potential or stored energy to actual or kinetic energy. To experience this just lift your arm straight out.

Now let it flop to your side. Aside from a little loss of energy due to air resistance, the increased speed of your falling arm is due to the transformation of the gravitational potential energy it had when it was held out. Thus, when a physicist says potential as in quantum potential or gravitational potential, he means stored energy capable of being converted.

Where is potential energy stored? Again physicists around Newton's time, borrowing on his genius, found an answer: in the field. In other words, they invented the concept of a field. Like a quantum wave function, it was spread out in space. There are two examples that you are probably familiar with: gravitational fields and electrical fields like those that surround high-tension power lines, producing that familiar sparking sound on damp days. By using the field concept, the physicist could keep his energy books in good order; all energy was conserved.

When we are dealing with small things like atoms, molecules, and electrons, we would also like energy to be conserved. The problem is that these particles don't behave as we might expect them to. For example, they vanish and reappear in unexpected places in violation of energy conservation rules. Physicist David Bohm found a way to get these particles to behave, at least theoretically. He did so by including along with all other forms of potential energy the particle might have, another form called the "quantum potential energy." This potential acted just like the other forms, but it did not depend on real fields like gravity and electrical fields (see G_2). Instead, the quantum potential depended on the magical quantum wave (see B_2) which, as you now know, moves faster than light. This meant instantaneous connection between any two points in space, thus breaking down the wall of light.

Thus, particles were now able to conserve energy whenever and however they moved, as well as affect things outside their own light cones (see F_1).

How can everything be connected? A recent article in *Scientific American* by Bernard d'Espagnat covers this exciting question with new theoretical findings from quantum physics and new experiments. D'Espagnat writes:

> The doctrine that the world is made up of objects whose existence is independent of human consciousness turns out to be in conflict with quantum mechanics and with facts established by experiment.

> BERNARD D'ESPAGNAT, "The Quantum Theory and Reality,"
> *Scientific American* (November 1979), p. 158.

Based upon an attempt by Einstein and his coworkers Podolsky and Rosen at Princeton University in 1935 to disprove quantum mechanics by showing that it predicts results in conflict with common sense (a strange argument coming from the trio, considering that it was Einstein's own relativity theory that was so hard to accept because it was in such conflict with accepted "common sense"), the physicist John Bell discovered a relationship (now called Bell's inequality) that showed conclusively that the results predicted by quantum mechanics contradict the principle of separability.

What is the principle of separability? Briefly, it states that things no longer in contact or communication with each other cannot affect one another. That means that whatever happens to one of these isolated things cannot and should not affect the behavior observed of the other thing. And guess what? Quantum mechanics violates this principle unashamedly. It points to a connectedness, a "quantum connectedness," which I call the Einstein connection. In other words, observations performed on one object can and do affect the results observed for another object, even when these objects are no longer in any known physical contact.

How can this happen? The simplest way I have of explaining this "connection" is through the faster-than-light quantum wave action (see B_2). However, because these waves describe only probabilities and not realities, the connection cannot be used under willful control; i.e., we cannot be sure of it. To create an Einstein connection between any two objects all that is necessary is that the two objects make contact and then separate. From the moment of contact on, any observations performed on one of the objects will alter the expected results for the other.

One of the most fascinating ideas to reach popularization from the world of general relativity is the black hole. It represents a place in space where space and time "fold over" on top of each other. The gravitational field surrounding the black hole is so intense that not only is all matter pulled into it, but even light cannot escape! Astronomers believe that certain stars that are "overweight" (i.e., have greater than a certain critical mass) can turn into black holes.

In the early 1960s, following up on an idea of Einstein and his coworker Rosen at Princeton University (as was becoming usual), several physicists, notably Martin Kruskal (also of Princeton) discovered that there was another side to a black hole! It was called the (did you guess it?) white hole. And it did play the opposite role. Everything came spewing out of it in a time-reversed sense. But the weirdest part of it was that the white hole and the black hole were not the same hole. Yet they were connected. If you were able to move faster than light, it would be possible to enter the black hole and instantly pop out of the white hole. It would be like walking into a room and finding, much to your amazement, that you had just emerged outside of it! Even more surprising, you could emerge at a place that was billions of light-years distant from the entry point. (Gosh, Toto, we're not in Kansas anymore.)

John Wheeler (the world-renowned physicist and former professor at Princeton) calls these black hole—white hole connections worm holes. Like worm holes underneath the soil, these "tubes" are underneath the "soil" of space-time.

John Wheeler and his coworkers created the idea of "quantum foam" (see reference to Wheeler). It's not the kind you brush your teeth with. Wheeler *et al.* envisioned that space-time spontaneously breaks down into, for want of a better picture, a foamy bubbliness, as we proceed to explore it on a very tiny, tiny level. That means exploring the smallest fractions of a second and the tiniest corners of space imaginable. If you were to cut one second in half and keep one half, throwing away the other, and then repeat this procedure 150 times, you would produce the smallest time interval physicists talk about. It is called the chronon. Furthermore, if you were to do this with one centimeter (about a third of an inch) and repeat your cutting 110 times, you would be down to the smallest piece of space physicists talk about. On this very tiny scale, some physicists think quantum physics and Einstein's general relativity, which includes gravity, intermingle producing quantum black holes (see I_1). These tiny holes or rips in space-time constitute a continual bubbliness which occurs spontaneously. It's as if the uncertainty principle (see A), which tries to keep matter from getting too well defined, i.e., too well located anywhere, and the enormous gravitational fields which would occur at such small distances, are in battle. The result? Quantum foam and just maybe the whole universe.

The oldest question ever asked may have been, "What is life?" Where is the line between living and nonliving things? I feel that there is no real boundary. The whole universe is alive, and because of the Einstein connection (see H) there is really only a one unbroken whole. When it is seen as parts we have the usual picture of the universe, in which we—you and I—play a seemingly small role.

One interesting ability of all living things is the ability to self-organize. But what is going on? What is self-organization? The answer is found in the familiar houseperson's dilemma: no matter how often (s)he cleans, the house gets dirty. Dirt is nothing more than things out of place; in other words, cleaning is restoring order and dirtying is destroying that order. Living things have a greater ability to "clean" than so-called nonliving things. The higher the consciousness of the "thing," the greater is its ability to "clean" itself. Life is the delicate balance between the forces of "dirt" and the forces of "clean." The higher on the scale of complexity this dividing line exists, the more "alive" the thing is. So-called inanimate objects may have lower dirt-clean boundary lines. (For more on interconnectedness and life's complexities, see note J₂.)

What determines the different degrees of consciousness? If everything is alive, why isn't everything equally conscious? One answer is complexity. We may simply be more complex than the rest of the universe and thereby more conscious, i.e., able to create more connections between events. An interesting slant toward this view is found in Everett's thesis (see E). He shows that complexity can be computed in terms of information theory. He calls this complexity, correlation. In other words, a correlation between any two things is a cooperative relation. This means that knowledge of one of the things tells you something about the other. Everett showed that the greater the numer of correlations, the larger is the information obtainable, i.e., the greater is the complexity. Everett then applied information theory to quantum physics and discovered that quantum interconnectedness (see H) creates correlations. Put simply, the more you interact with the universe, the more you know, and Everett shows us why this is so.

A further discovery, found by Everett (see E and J_2), was that refinement produces greater complexity and therefore more information. This arises because, as a result of refinement, more correlations can occur and thus a more enriched observation of life can occur. What is refinement? To give an example, perhaps an obvious one, consider a room full of people. The lights are out and no one is allowed to speak or touch the others present. What can we say about this room? The answer is, it's full of people. Now keeping the lights off and without making any sounds, let the people touch each other in a "group grope." Now what can we say? The interactions between the folks certainly produced more information. For example, we now know that there are males and females present. After a while, the room's distribution of people will change to reflect the attractions and repulsions felt by those people for each other. Feeling is a refinement in the distribution. By turning on the lights, we learn much more. Seeing produces even greater refinement. It allows for another kind of interaction to be present, that produced by light. If the people begin to speak to each other, we learn a great deal more. Now the room may divide into regions of like peoples, those that see things in a similar way, those that feel similarly about each other, etc. But, can we go on refining *ad infinitum* (without end)?

The answer appears to be no. There is a limit to refinement and it is due to the uncertainty principle (see A). We may be the perfection of the universe. Further refinement would not produce any more perfected beings. Thus evolution may be just changing the form, enjoying more of the complexities which have been present since the beginning.

The nonabsoluteness of time and space was replaced by the idea of the absoluteness of space-time. Put simply, space and time are linked together and are interchangeable. The connection between space and time, however, is not apparent unless you are dealing with vast distances, very short times, or things moving very near to the speed of light. It is on these scales that relativity makes its presence known to us. For example, we have discovered that no object can move faster than light, by examining large distances (sending radio signals to Voyager and receiving them when it was near Jupiter took forty minutes one way or eighty minutes round trip). This finite limit imposed a new meaning to communication and therefore to what we mean by things happening at the same time anywhere in the universe. This new meaning of simultaneity, in turn, showed that what we meant by *now* was not universal. In other words my "now" is not your "now" unless we happen to be moving at the same speed and in the same direction. If not, our "nows" are not the same. This led to moving clocks going slower than stationary clocks and moving rulers foreshortening when compared to nonmoving ones. The time discrepancy between the clocks "became" a spatial distance, namely the distance the object moved in the time measured by the stationary clock. Similarly, the discrepancy in length of the moving ruler "transformed" into a time, the time it would take to move the ruler's length at the speed of light. In this way space-time became absolute, because we could always account for the discrepancy by changing the appropriate time into space or space into time. This procedure for accounting was in practice no more difficult than changing dollars into quarters and quarters into dollars. Relativity and the role played by light's speed provided the understanding that space and time separately were simply different units for the exchange of space-time.

These fundamental interchanges also occur in a gravitational field (see G_2 for the idea of a field). In other words, clocks in a strong gravitational field tick more slowly than clocks in a weak field. Similarly distances foreshorten* in the direction of a strong gravitational field as compared to no field present. We normally don't notice our clocks slowing in a gravitational field, but physicists Pound and Rebka did, in a remarkable experiment at Harvard University. They were able to detect the difference in time rates for two "atomic clocks" when one was placed in the basement and the other on an elevated floor of a building. The basement clock was "ticking" more slowly because it was held in a more intense gravitational field (nearer the earth's center) than the other one.

How big is space? Does it go on forever? Einstein not only illuminated these matters, he showed us how to give meaning to these questions! We must be objective and tell how we propose to experience the answers. It's not enough to just romanticize. If we can imagine going on a space exploration journey, we will find that space has no fixed determined size!! The size of space demands on us. It depends on how fast we move through it. The faster we go, the shorter the travel time and distance. This is because moving clocks go slow and moving lengths are foreshortened along the travel direction, according to relativity (see note K). For example, the distance between the earth and the sun is about 93 million miles. It takes light just under 500 seconds to make the journey, according to our observations on earth. What would happen if you were to make the journey? The time it would take you, of course, would depend on how fast you flew, but relativity

*The space around you compresses as you fall into a black hole! See Ronald Gautreau and Banesh Hoffman's article in the *Physical Review D*, 1978.

has some surprises as you approach the speed of light. Suppose you were to rocket from the earth to the sun at 10 percent light-speed. Your journey would take 5,000 seconds (about eighty-three minutes). But as you increase your speed, the journey time decreases faster than you might expect. At 71 percent light-speed, your journey takes 500 seconds, the same time it takes light as observed by those back on earth. At 94 percent light-speed you're only in the ship 180 seconds (three minutes). And at 99 percent light-speed, it takes you only one minute to reach the sun!* Finally, if you were able to fly at light-speed itself, you would literally be there the same time you left! Vast though the universe may appear to us mortals, it is nothing for light to travel through it. At light-speed, all travel times are reduced to nothing.

Another way to view this is to imagine yourself at rest in your spaceship and see the whole universe rushing by you. Thus, you would see the earth leave you and the sun approach you. The earth-sun distance would make a very large ruler and, as you now know, moving rulers shrink in length (see K). Since this large "ruler" is now passing by you at 99 percent light-speed, it has shrunk to only sixty light-seconds in length, or just over 11 million miles. Speed up and you can reduce this distance to under one foot in length! So, how big is space? As big as we think it. If we think at the speed of light, space is reduced to the size of a pinpoint!

By using our minds we can imagine such a space and still know this whole universe just as we see it to be.

*Remember that space and time are relative to the observer. Even though your clock on the ship has only ticked off one minute, the folks back home on earth, who remain at rest compared to you, would say that you were gone for just over eight minutes.

"Discovering the universe in a grain of sand"—how often have you heard that and wondered just what it meant? How can a part of the universe contain the whole? I think I first felt this when traveling around the world in the early 1970s. I became aware that people were very much the same and that cultures were coatings over human values, the same values I had. Through other experiences I have come to see not only people this way, but animals as well. In fact, when I look closely enough, even plants exhibit attributes that I can hardly separate from my own. I mention these observations as obvious ways to experience a whole truth, one which is apparently true for all living things. Since the boundary between life an nonlife is virtually nonexistent (see J_1, J_2 and J_3), these discoveries, I believe, are universal.

Physicists have come to understand this in terms of the Einsten connection (see H) and the hologram. The hologram is a remarkable invention that makes use of a rather sophisticated and fascinating property of all waves: they have amplitudes and phases. The amplitude of a wave measures its strength. The phase of the wave determines its rhythmic relationship with all other waves. When waves in phase add together coherently they form a single wave with dramatic strength. Two waves in phase create a wave with four times the strength of a single wave. Three "in-phase" waves create a single wave with nine times the strength of one wave, and so on. Using light waves scientists have been able to record on film the interference patterns produced by an object when that object reflects the powerful energy of a laser. The recorded pattern that results whenever the reflected waves from the object and the original laser light waves are combined in space is called a hologram. The film records the complicated ripple pattern in the same manner as an ordinary film emulsion records the light in a photographic negative. When the laser light is passed through the emulsion once again, a rather amazing optical illusion is generated. By looking through the flat emulsion plate, you are able to see the image as if you were looking at the object through a window. The actual object has long been removed, of course.

Even more amazing is what occurs if you destroy the hologram itself by cutting it into smaller pieces like a broken windowpane. If you look through any of the pieces in the same way, you will again see the whole image of the object reconstructed. It is a weaker image, but nevertheless a completely reconstructed view. The amazing hologram not only gives you a three-dimensional image of the object, but also enables you to see this image as if you were actually looking at the real object. For example, if you were to move your head, changing the point of view, your picture of the real object would change. Exactly the same thing occurs when you are looking at a holographic image; turn your head and you see a different side of the three-dimensional object's image.

This is what we mean by the part contains the whole. The piece of the hologram contains the whole image. Perhaps the universe is a gigantic space-time hologram made up of interfering quantum waves (see B_2) just like a laser's light waves. Each grain of sand holds the image of the whole universe.

John Wheeler and Richard Feynman (Nobel Prize-winning physicist from the California Institute of Technology) developed the idea that all of the particles in the universe could be reduced to one single particle. For example, take an electron. This tiny bit of electricity is responsible not only for the structure of atoms and molecules, but for the human nervous system. Without it bouncing back and forth, all chemical activity would come to a screeching halt. Electrons banging into the back of your television screen produce the tiny light bursts that reach your retina with the evening news. How could there be only one electron in the whole universe?

The answer is: it must be allowed to travel back in time! If it can do this little trick, it can then appear in two or more places at the same time. In a similar manner, it could appear in a very large number of places at the same time and make up a whole universe of electrons. Suppose you could travel back in time for just ten seconds. Could you appear, really appear, in two places at the same time? To see how, imagine that you have just entered a room from a doorway and taken a seat. Suppose that now, just now, you got up from your seat and walked to another doorway and exited, with a slight difference: the clocks ticked backward for ten seconds. How would this scene look to bystanders?

Do you see it yet? Suppose that you first entered the room at ten seconds to one. At one o'clock you got up and walked out another door, arriving there at ten seconds before you left your seat. Although your actions would seem innocuous to you, to everyone else in that room the scene would be bizarre, because they would see you standing at both doorways at ten seconds to one; in other words, you would be in two places at the same time. This is what we mean by the drawing on p. 45. The spiral is winding backward in time.

The speculation that matter may be nothing but trapped light energy arises from the famous Einstein formula, $E = Mc^2$, which equates energy, E, and matter, M, by multiplying the latter by the speed of light, c, twice. Physicists have observed this formula in action in the process known as electron-position annihilation and in the inverse process known as electron-positron creation. What happens is that an electron (see M_2) collides with its antimatter self, the positron, and both vanish, leaving two particles of light called photons instead. It is this property of positrons that gave us the idea that they were antimatter. If the light energy is high enough, the photons can be turned back into matter and antimatter again. But there is more to our story, for how does light get trapped?

How does light get itself trapped? The answer is gravity. If the gravitational field is large enough, light gets bent by it. By bent light I mean that it no longer moves in a straight line but follows a curved one instead. The stronger the gravitational field (see G_2 for the idea of a field), the more light bends. Finally, if the field is sufficiently strong, the light bends into a circle. And guess where gravity gets that strong. Did you guess it? Yes, indeed, in a black hole.

Following on Wheeler's idea of quantum foam (see I_2) consisting of spontaneously occurring miniblack holes and white holes, we may envision this foam as entrapping light in its bubbles. These tiny gaps in space-time generate very strong gravitational fields over very, very small distances. At the center of these bubbles are points called singularities, singular points in space-time where forces are beyond comprehension. It is because of these tiny "beyond space-time" points that gravity can entrap light. I speculate that perhaps the stable particles of matter are those with just the right light energy in the traps; too much and the "hole" decays into other particles, too little and the light energy gets scattered by "holes."

If the bubble is rotating, these singular points "bloom out" into rings. And these rings can lead into other amazing adventures, like travels to other universes. (See P_1.)

After Martin Kruskal and others developed mathematical solutions for what goes on in a black hole (see I_1), many scientists became interested in general relativity and in particular in the subject of what goes on inside black holes. Do things change if the hole has an electrical charge? What happens if the hole is rotating? In 1963 Australian mathematician Roy P. Kerr found out. He developed solutions for a rotating black hole. He found that with rotation, the "hole" had a structure. This structure is shown on p. 48. If miniblack holes are like the Kerr black hole, they would show a similar structure.

What happens inside the black hole? As we approach the outermost zone, which is called the static limit, we notice some strange goings-on. Any light we happen to be emitting is being "swept away" in the direction of rotation of the hole. It's as if a giant invisible wind were blowing the light around the hole. As we move inside the static limit, we find ourselves in what is called the ergosphere. It is an energetic zone where light is both swept around and gravitationally pulled toward the hole's center. If we were somehow caught in this region, we would still be able to escape, even though the field is very large. In fact, it is possible to "farm" this region and extract energy from it. If a falling spaceship entered the ergosphere and were to break in two, part would be ejected with more energy than it had going in and the other part would be captured by the hole. This is called the Penrose mechanism after Roger Penrose who discovered it.

Next we cross the outer event horizon. In the region bounded by this sphere and another sphere called the inner event horizon, space and time have turned topsyturvy. In this zone there is no turning back, we must go on. Now if the hole were for any reason to stop rotating, we would be in a terrible mess! We would crash into the singularity at the center of the hole (see O). But we are lucky, the hole is rotating, so instead we are about to take an amazing journey! As soon as we cross the inner event horizon, space and time reverse again and the world becomes normal. We may stay here awhile and not feel compelled to enter the singularity. In fact, we can leave the hole! We simply head outward, passing once again through the inner event horizon into the topsy-turvy region between horizons. This time we will be compelled to move outward across the outer event horizon, where once again space and time reverse and become normal. However, we won't have returned to our own universe, necessarily. In fact, it appears that we will have journeyed to another universe parallel to our own. This new universe may be our own at an earlier time in its evolution. This is what we mean by a time machine.

The unique feature of all black holes is the one-way-ness of the event horizons surrounding them (see P$_1$). Once you cross the boundary, space and time reverse, trapping you and making you move onward in space in as compelling a manner as you are presently made to move onward in time! You are now, so to speak, caught in the time stream; never can you "turn around" and reach yesterday. Perhaps the tiny black holes are generating this flow of time, and perhaps that is why we cannot go back in time. I think of these tiny rips in space-time as little time suckers, sucking in the very fabric of space-time, indeed the threads of time that weave it all together.

In the drawing (p. 50) we see the future being pulled into the black hole. From our vantage point, being made up of these tiny rips, we are moving into the future. We remain outside of the static limit and event horizons, so nothing unusual is going on. But if we were to cross over, through both outer and inner event horizons, we would find things had reversed. Instead of being pulled back into the hole, we would be compelled to move onward and outward, passing through the outer event horizon (once we have crossed the inner one) into another universe. Thus white holes gush us out, while black holes suck us in. On the white hole side we would experience the past being pulled past us into the white hole. For us, the universe would appear to be running backward in time, if this universe were our own. However, it need not be ours at all; it could be a parallel universe having its own sense of time, flowing opposite to our own but nevertheless in a perfectly reasonable way for those who live in it.

Antimatter—even the name gives us shivers! Whenever an object collides with its mirror-image antimatter partner, the two objects vanish in a puff of great light energy (see

I_1). For example, the antimatter partner for the electron (see M_2) is called the positron. It has properties very similar to those of an electron, with one outstanding exception: everything is reversed! The electrical charge of the electron is negative, while the position has a positive charge (hence its name). The positron's spin direction is opposite to the electron's. Does it also have a negative mass?

No. It has positive mass, but it can annihilate its partner along with itself. One explanation for this disappearing trick would be for it to be its own partner traveling backward in time (see M_2). This would enable it to be in two places at the same time, but in one of those places it would be moving in the opposite time direction. To us who are flowing toward the future, it would then appear as a particle with just the opposite properties we observe for electrons. But how can it flow in the opposite direction?

I speculate that the answer lies in the white hole. We now know that whenever a black hole forms, a white hole must form too, at least theoretically. The only problem is that we may not be in any position to observe it. That's because we are already in a time stream, we are already participating in a universe. If we could get beyond space-time and have a look-see, we would observe the whole time-space history of our universe and indeed of other universes that are connected to ours. In note I_1, I talked about the parallel universe discovered by Martin Kruskal and others. One of the interesting features of this "other" universe, which is connected to our own through the singular regions bounded by the event horizon, is that its time sense runs exactly opposite to our own. Thus, what is future for us appears to be past for them and vice versa. If we could somehow "leak through the barrier" connecting these universes (which for nonspinning holes would require us to move faster than light), we would find that all processes would be proceeding backward in comparison with our own time sense. This wouldn't mean anything strange to the inhabitants of this other universe, however. For them everything would be proceeding normally, but for us it would appear just like a movie run backward.

But this is just what is required, for there to be antimatter!

149

We would be antimatter in their universe, and they would be antimatter in ours. Is the white hole a unit of antimatter? No, but through the white hole—black hole—worm hole connection, antimatter could enter our universe. This could occur if the hole is spinning (see P_2).

Not only do rotating black holes have positive mass, they can also exhibit negative mass! To observe this we must approach the ring singularity and bravely jump through the hoop. Here we enter perhaps the strangest universe of all. Everything is topsy-turvy. Even the gravity that was pulling us into the ring becomes repulsive as we cross through. Once on the other side, we are in what is called negative space. In this region gravity behaves in an opposite manner. It repulses or pushes other particles away. The inside of the hole is behaving as if it had negative mass.

If space-time does spontaneously break down into black hole—white hole—worm hole pairs on the scale of a quantum foam (see I_2), it should also be possible to create very short-lived negative mass regions too! Some physicists speculate that negative mass can act in a screening capacity, thus weakening the force of gravity. Perhaps gravity is much stronger on this scale and what we experience in our everyday world are the leftovers of this constant battle between gravity and the uncertainty principle (see I_2).

The Penrose diagram on p. 55 is a handy tool for looking at space-time from a vantage point which is beyond space-time. The two square areas joined at one corner represent two parallel universes for a nonrotating black hole—white hole. Let us assume that we live in the right-hand universe. If we could live forever, we would appear as a line starting at the lower infinity boundary line and passing in time (note the time's arrow) to the upper infinity boundary line; that is, provided we didn't stray too close to the event horizon of the black hole, which as we see could lie in our future. If we crossed this horizon, we would be doomed to hit the singularity, shown as the wavy line and labeled black hole singularity.

On the other hand, if we were in the left-hand universe, our history would take us down the diagram toward the white hole singularity. We wouldn't be in communication with the "other" universe, so we wouldn't have any reason to suspect that anything is weird. The right-hand and left-hand universes have opposite flows (see P_2 and P_3).

The search for fundamental building blocks has currently led to the idea of quarks, tiny constituents of the protons of any atom. As remarkable as these particles may be, someone will eventually seek to discover what quarks are made of. How far down the scale of space-time shall we seek? Perhaps there are really only two different "forces" at work: the quantum force operating through uncertainty, keeping things from being pinned down; and the gravitational force showing itself as an organizational force, pulling the fabric of space-time together into masses, the organizational units we call particles.

Perhaps the universe is the battleground between these two forces, and perhaps the remarkable properties we discover are the compromises between these two combatants. As I see it, we have a double flow from beyond space-time and back again. Between the two streams, universes are created and destroyed. This creates the turbulence of the quantum foam and the structures we call matter.

What are paranormal phenomena? Many scientists do not believe there is any such thing as psychokinesis, bending light by thought, materialization and dematerialization, astral travel, out-of-body travel, clairvoyance and precognition, reincarnation, auric fields around living things, telepathy, psychometry, teleportation, levitation, healing with the mind or hands, or anything at all like a higher consciousness. It is perhaps not an overstatement to say that little or no *scientific* evidence exists for any of the above. Yet we have multitudes of people, cultures, and institutes studying such phenomena with great zeal. I must admit that a universe without such things would be a dull place to live in, at least it would be dull for me. So why doesn't science do something to either disprove or prove such phenomena? The answer could lie in the methods used by science. The chief criterion of any scientific evidence is that it be repeatable and demonstrable. In other words it must be objectively observed. Many of the above paranormalities are quite subjective and depend on the state of the observer.

In this book, I felt that such phenomena deserve at least a theoretical look. I feel that the barrier between physics and psychology must come down. Thus, my commentary points to what I think is a plausible explanation of such phenomena.

In a delightful little book by George Gamow, *Mr. Tomkins in paperback,* our hero, an ordinary bank clerk, meets the paradoxical worlds of modern physics face to face. In one adventure he meets a character called Maxwell's Demon in a glass of water. Having shrunk to atomic size, Mr. Tomkins finds the demon at work, busily batting molecules of water from one place to another with his tennis racket. With a penchant for accuracy, the demon persists in hitting all of the sluggishly moving molecules to one region of the glass and carefully holding his position against the faster moving molecules by keeping them at bay in a separate region. The result of his handiwork? The ice cold water begins to boil! The demon had carefully corralled the speedsters very near the surface and all were moving upward and escaping. This little adventure taught our hero about the connection between entropy and energy; in this case, heat energy.

There are two kinds of energy in the world, useful and nonuseful. According to the first law of thermodynamics, there are no limitations on the possibility of transforming energy from one form to another. Our little friend, the Maxwell Demon, is not in violation of this law as he bats the molecules around with his tiny racket. On the basis of the first law alone it is perfectly possible for the demon to transform heat—which he is so carefully doing by selectively choosing the molecular balls he hits—into work. This work appears as the boiling of the ice cold water. In fact the more the water boils the colder will the water become because the demon is taking heat from the water in order to make it boil.

Since there is a practically unlimited supply of heat energy contained in the soil, the water and the atmosphere, it would be possible, according to the first law alone, to build a machine which would transform this heat into work, and therefore useful energy. If this were so, the energy crunch would be over. As long as the sun shines there is heat. And as long as there is heat there will be unlimited useful energy.

But there is something else going on. It is called the second law of thermodynamics. According to this law it is not possible to transform heat from a body at a given temperature to another body at a higher temperature. Another way this law is stated is that it is not possible to just transform heat into work without some heat energy becoming unavailable for work. In other words there will always be some heat energy which will not be useful. If the first body is colder than the second body then all of the first body's heat is nonuseful with regard to doing work by passing its heat to the second body.

Ludwig Boltzmann discovered a way to measure just

how much nonuseful energy there would be. His measure was called the entropy of the system. Whenever heat energy was transformed the entropy of the system undergoing the transformation was found to always increase or at least remain constant. An increase in entropy meant that some of the heat energy was unavailable—never to be regained without expending even more energy to get it back. Boltzmann discovered that the entropy was also a measure of the amount of disorder found in the system.

Disorder can be defined mathematically. It is the number of arrangements of different objects in which no two arrangements differ from each other in any essential way. Thus an arrangement of four coins in which there are two heads and two tails showing is more disordered than an arrangement of the coins with four heads showing. This is because there are six ways to arrange four coins (by flipping them around) so that two heads and two tails show while there is only one way to show them all heads.

The higher the disorder the higher the entropy and the more nonuseful energy is created in the transformation.

Can thoughts cause a violation of the second law of thermodynamics? Early work on information theory indicates that information about something acts very much like entropy. The reason appears to be that both entropy and information depend on order—the higher the order the more information it contains. Conversely the higher the disorder the less information it contains. The little Maxwell Demon is imparting his knowledge to the molecular balls as he bats them around. This is because he is consciously choosing just when to bat a ball. If we take into account both the entropy of the ice cold and yet boiling water and the information entropy of the Demon, it is found that the total entropy *will* increase. Thus acting together, the second law of thermodynamics will not be violated by the Demon *and* the water. The Demon's thoughts are in a sense transforming the energy, making more of it available than there would be if the Demon was unconscious. Perhaps human beings are capable of acting in a like manner. Perhaps human thought—through the process of observation (see B_1)—can make heat flow from a cold body to a hot body in apparent violation of the second law. It would not actually violate that law when the entropy of the human thought was taken into account.

Can consciousness move through a black hole? Can you dream of being a Stone Age observer and actually be back in the Stone Age? Can you then return to the present by just waking up? Well, there is no scientific evidence for any of the above, so skeptics rest assured. However, out-of-body experience has been reported by many people. Can we be sure that our dreams take place just in our heads? Perhaps our dreams take us to places we can't go to in our bodies. Perhaps we are tuning in to other worlds parallel to this one. There are dreams and there are dreams. Not all are the same. In some you may be able to consciously direct your own actions. Perhaps time travel, space travel and out-of-body experience can be related. If our thoughts are carried by quantum waves (see B_2 for definition and properties), there is no logical reason why they could not travel outward or inward, seeking the nearest black hole exit points to parallel worlds—worlds which may be our own in the past or future. If our thoughts were carried by quantum waves, they could move to edges of the universe and back again faster than light. In an exciting paper by Benford, Book, and Newcomb ("The Tachyonic Anti-Telephone," *Physical Review D*, Vol. 2, 1970, p. 263), the authors show how a faster-than-light signal carrying information could be "reflected" backward in time. If such a signal existed and if the future were completely determined, such information could explain precognition. However, the universe doesn't seem to be predetermined, at least in any ordinary meaning of the term (see T_1).

155

What does it mean to know something? Until the discoveries of quantum physics, knowledge and reality were thought to be completely separate, provided that by reality we mean physical reality. The study of what we *think* about reality is called epistemology. What actually *is* reality is the central question of ontology. Quantum physics led to the remarkable connection between these two methods of thought. It showed us that in principle we cannot separate them, even if we do so in practice. Thus, if we continue to hold them as dogmatically separate, we must ultimately lie about the universe. So then, what is the truth?

It appears safe to say that knowing is disrupting. To learn anything, we have to alter things in irreversible ways. We can never return to what we had before. Thus, an oracle who sees the past or future of any individual is not just objectively seeing what's there, he must be creating it as well. That is why we have probable life and not actual life indicated in the drawing on p. 74.

Are the basic building blocks of the universe the same today as they were yesterday? Is an atom of hydrogen identical throughout all time? Some physicists think that not only is the universe evolving and expanding, but the so-called constants of the physical universe are also slowly changing. For example, the charge of electricity carried by an electron may have increased in time and the gravitational constant weakened in time (see the article, "The Cosmical Mystery—The Relationship Between Microphysics and Cosmology," by Roxburgh in *The Encyclopedia of Ignorance*, New York: Pergamon Press, 1977). This means that electrical forces have gotten stronger and gravitational forces weaker throughout history. Could my atoms remember these changes? Perhaps reincarnation is such a memory, the past information flashing before our minds whenever quantum waves (see B_2) from our past produce interference patterns with our present quantum waves, in much the same manner as two sound waves with different frequencies make beats in our ears. The past electron's wave would be slightly out of beat with the present electron's wave due to the particle having a slightly stronger electrical charge today than yesterday.

What is memory? In a sense, all laws of conservation, such as the law of the conservation of energy (see G_1), are the universe's memory. It remembers how much energy it had before, after, and possibly during any interactions among things. If memory is somehow "stored energy" or potential energy, then a change in the forces that bind us together, i.e., the electrical and gravitational forces (perhaps also the nuclear forces), could cause memory flashes.

Are there auric fields surrounding living things? Why can't we see them? Why do some people see auras and others not? What causes auras? First of all, I don't think that auras exist in the same way that electrical fields and gravitational fields exist. If they are real, they are more in the eyes of the beholder than actually surrounding the person who has the aura. Yet people who see auras are able to tell when the person who has the aura changes his thought pattern (thinks an angry thought or a very sexy thought, for example). No obvious change takes place on the person's face or body movement, so what is going on? I suspect that auras have something to do with the quantum wave function which not only exists in our minds and brains but also exists in space-time (see B_2). Perhaps the aura is the visual imprinting, on the retinas of the observer, of the quantum wave pops taking place in the observed person's mind (see F_2). When the person changes his mind, it instantly changes the quantum wave between the observer and the observed. The observer who is sensitive to this change could know about it through one of his own five senses. For example, he might smell something, or see a glow of purple. Or he might hear voices or feel a foreign presence. For someone who has a well-developed thinking mind—that is, a person who is very facile with words—these quantum wave pops might appear as thoughts or sudden feelings about the observed ("I know you are angry," for example). The feeling you may sometimes have that you know someone you have never met, could be a matter of tuning into the person's quantum wave pops.

The Einstein connection (see H) could explain how people can know things about other people that are beyond normal communication. However, there are two ends to this "mind-link." Furthermore, the two persons involved in such a link are each free to pursue thoughts that would unlink the link! This is due to the uncertainty principle and the complementarity of choice (see A and B_1). To establish a link, the persons would have had to interact in some way at an earlier time. This is called correlating their quantum wave functions (see J_2). The two people would not have had to meet, so long as there was some connection between them in the past; for example, a mutual friend who had contacted both people at an earlier time.

Can this connection be used to send a signal from one person to the other? I don't think that it can, because this channel violates what appears to be necessary for transfer of information: the signal must travel at light-speed or less. Since this involves faster-than-light movement, it cannot be used for information transfer that is willed at either end of the link. This doesn't mean that each person cannot know something that is occurring for the other. If a laser on the moon shines beams at the earth, it is certainly possible for two people at opposite ends of the world to see these beams at the same time.

"Beam me down, Scotty!" I must admit to being a "Star-Trek" trekkie. The thought that someday we may be able to cause a giant quantum jump (see F_2), allowing us to move matter on a large scale as quickly as it appears to move on an atomic scale, excites me. Could we find the way? How do we search for a method? Perhaps it is possible to create a holographic pattern of a large-scale object using quantum waves instead of light waves. If this pattern could be stored in one location (I don't know how) and a quantum wave beam somehow created (again, don't ask me how), maybe we could reconstruct an image of a thing that would recreate itself as an object. (For a description of a hologram, see M_1.)

How does an object vanish here and appear there? One idea is that time has another dimension to it. We call this time imaginary or i-time, and we imagine i-time to be somehow running crosswise to real time, much as the length of the room you are sitting in runs crosswise to the width of the room. Scientists who perform calculations which involve chemical reactions depending on the movement of an electron (called charge transfer reactions) often use i-time in their calculations. Imagine an object that moves from here to there in space and in i-time, but not in real time. To observers caught in the stream of real time, such a movement would appear as a giant quantum jump, taking place in no time at all.

I love magic shows and have performed as a magician myself. Watching a levitation act, I have always been mystified. Can a person somehow tap the secret trick of the universe and just float off the ground? How could this be done? Well, if the quantum foam is made of tiny black hole—white hole—worm hole pairs with both positive and negative mass parts (see P_4 and p. 51), perhaps it is possible to use our thoughts to line up the bubbles so that the negative mass holes temporarily come together, thus lifting us up.

Healing, the dream of the physician to make us well, derives from the word *whole*. Thus, to be healed is to be "wholed," at one with the universe. We speak of a loving hand, a sympathetic heart. Sympathy is a rhythmic understanding. A sympathetic person feels what the other person is feeling. Perhaps healing is a phase harmony (see M_1) of our quantum waves. By being together with each other we enhance this harmony, just as when two pieces of a broken hologram are put together the image seen is stronger. (Also see H.)

In this view, illness is just vibration out of harmony. Illness is created in the same way that anything is created: it arises out of thought. I think that thoughts "interfere" with the universe, disturb the universe. However, don't let these thoughts disturb you; you really can't help disturbing the universe. That is the only way to learn about it. Thus, illness is a way of learning about yourself.

Is there a higher consciousness? Can we unite with it, become aware of its presence? Throughout history human beings have dreamed and hoped to unite with their God, whatever that God is called. Perhaps that unity is related to the quantum or Einstein connection between us all. Certainly quantum physics has broadened our viewpoint.

How, then, do we do it? How can we learn to feel this connection? How can we become more intelligent, more sensitive, and more understanding of ourselves and the universe we live in? The answer is simple. First, we must choose between alternatives. Do we really want to be more intelligent? Is greater sensitivity something we all desire? Do we wish to understand the universe we live in? If a yes answer to these questions is important to you, you are already in contact with higher consciousness. If, on the other hand, these ideas are not important to you, there will be no awareness of higher consciousness reaching you. The choice is not with "it," it is with you. To hear the news, you must turn the receiver on. To turn it on, you must first want to hear the news.

I believe that the process of "tuning" to higher consciousness is one of greater-self-reflection (see C).

What is energy? We have already looked at some consequences of energy (see notes G_1, G_2, G_3, and R_2). Although physicists know a great deal about energy, they don't know what it is really (see, for example, Ch. 4 in Vol. 1 of *The Feynman Lectures on Physics,* by Feynman, Leighton and Sands, Addison-Wesley Publishing Co., Massachusetts, 1963). We do know however, that whatever it is, it can be calculated and conserved; in other words, we know how to use it, lose it, and hold on to it. One of its interesting properties is that it easily changes its form or structure. For example, by sending electricity through a thin wire, we can turn electrical energy into heat energy and light energy. The common protocell that operates by circulating an electric current, changes light energy into electrical energy. A falling object is constantly converting potential gravitational energy into kinetic or moving energy. When the object hits the ground the kinetic energy changes into heat and sound energy. It would not be an oversimplification to say that energy is doing-ness.

Thought takes energy. Could thought be energy? Could consciousness itself be pure energy? Perhaps the many forms of energy are similar to the many forms of consciousness. We have known since the discovery of Einstein's famous $E = Mc^2$ formula, that mass, M, and energy, E, are just different structures of energy. Perhaps all of the different forms in the universe are just different forms of consciousness manifesting as observers and things observed.

Perhaps the universe is just one big dance. If quantum waves are the basis for all matter and consciousness, then it is reasonable to say that rhythm is necessary. For all waves must have periodic or rhythmic movement. Since the quantum wave flows faster than light (see B_2), all time is involved.

One of the most difficult things to imagine is an infinite universe. How can it just go on forever? But perhaps even more difficult is to conceive of a finite universe. What happens at the edge of it? What's on the other side of the boundary?

No one really knows, for it appears to be impossible to visualize anything in more than three dimensions, and as we know the universe exists in the domain of four dimensions: three of space and one of time. However, if we use our imaginations for a moment and imagine the universe existing only in two space dimensions and one time dimension, it is possible to visualize it. To do this, imagine the whole universe existing on the surface of a balloon. What can we understand from this simple model?

One question is, does it go on forever? In a sense, from our viewpoint, it does not. Yet even if you were to move on this sphere continually in the same direction, you would not reach any edge. Our universe seems to have this same property. But hold on, you may say; if you walk around the balloon, won't you come back to the same place you started from? Well, yes, if the balloon is not expanding or contracting. But if someone is blowing it up, you will not come back to the same point even though it will appear similar. That's because of the added time dimension. Our universe also exhibits this feature, that it is expanding.

Thus the universe is not contained in anything; it contains itself. But, you add, that's easy for us to see in the case of a balloon, because we are standing outside of the balloon. Yes, indeed, from our vantage point, which is beyond space and time, it is quite clear what is going on. That is what we mean when we say that space and time do not exist at higher levels. We make the analogy to the balloon universe. If space and time were confined to the expanding balloon, you who were watching it expand would be in a higher space, beyond space-time.

What is will? How do we humans possess the ability to choose what we want? Recent research by L. Bass in Australia* connects quantum mechanics with willpower. Will appears to be nothing but choice acting on a very small atomic level. Quantum physics points to complementary attributes of reality (see B_1). In such a situation you can't have both attributes at the same time. The act of getting one destroys the ability to get the other. Thus, although you want to float in the air, it may not be possible because you are trying to defeat the principle of complementarity. Of course, the usual explanation is that gravity holds you down.

In the Everett picture of quantum mechanics (see E), all realities are equally possible, even those in which you float. Although all of these realities are equally possible, there are more realities occurring in which you don't float. Since these realities occur more often, they can conspire to produce a least action path (see note Z). Our minds may be constructed to only pay the most attention to the least action paths of these realities. Thus we experience this reality rather than one in which we float.

If, as Everett puts it, you exist in all parallel universes at the same time, you could also be happier in some and sadder in others than you feel right now. Perhaps your

*Bass is with the Department of Mathematics at the University of Queensland. This relates to work he did in 1975, published in the journal *Foundations of Physics*.

thoughts and imaginings are your awareness of those other parallel universes. The question is, can we change reality by our thoughts?

Our view of ourselves is changing. In the classical Newtonian picture human beings had no special place in the universe. They were simply observers. What happened outside of them could only change by external forces and their consequences. Given the exact location and momentum of each and every object in the universe and all of the forces acting upon these objects, everything that occurred in the future was completely predictable. If human will also fell into that picture, then even human behavior was completely predictable. This left no room for free will. In such a universe everything was predetermined. Not only was the future predetermined but also the past. In other words, it would be possible to know with absolute certainty all that went before as well as all that would come after.

In the twentieth-century "quantum" view, particularly before 1935, we found out that we could not know the position and momentum of each and every object in the universe. We were not limited by ignorance, however, but by a new discovery in physics. This was the discovery of the quantum nature of all things. It said that at best all we could hope to discover was the probable location and momentum of each and every object. It also showed us that there was a connection between the probable location and the probable momentum of an object. This connection was based upon a discovery called the principle of uncertainty (see A). It showed that any experiment that determined the location of an object exactly had to leave the experimenter in complete doubt as to its future location. This doubt was due to the total loss of information concerning the object's momentum which had to take place when the object's position was measured. By softening the measurement precision, so that the object's position was "blurry" and therefore not well determined, the next "blurry" position was able to be predicted. Thus, by giving up information about location we were able to gain some about the next location, or in other words we were able to learn a little about its momentum. This blurry picture of objects was thought to be more of a nuisance than a fundamental restriction placed upon matter. Again, the human observer played no special role. The world was simply just a little more complicated than the Newtonian picture had indicated.

Since 1935, our views have changed more towards the idea that somehow the observer enters the picture. It is not completely clear how this happens, however. One way to include the observer was found in Richard Feynman's "path-integral" development of quantum mechanics. In this picture every possible path that an object could follow in reaching a given location in the future is considered. Uncertainty then developed "naturally" because we would not be able to say for certain which path the object would actually take. Like a detective story where all the characters are suspects, each and every path plays a role in the final act of observation. Even though all paths are equally "suspect," some of the paths are seen to conspire in a particularly "incriminating" manner. These paths "stand out" from the rest because they cluster around one particular path, called "the least action path."

What's so special about "the least action path"? It is special because it is so ordinary. Any object following the least action path appears to fit our classical Newtonian picture of how an object "should" behave. In other words, an object on a least action path has a very normal history. For example, we can predict where it was in the past and where it will go in the future. It is a "good" law-abiding object. It follows the cause-effect rule.

What happens if there is more than one least action path? (Several paths can be least if they are all equal.) Then the object behaves as if it followed all the least action paths. In fact, if all possible paths are least action paths, the object ceases to move from one place to another like an ordinary object. Instead it moves like a wave, spreading out in space until the moment of truth when it is observed. Every path, least action or not, contributes to the spread. At the instant of observation, the spreading stops.

And that is when, as I see it, the observer enters the scene. Each minuscule "act of observation" reduces the polyphony of paths to just one point on one path. As if by magic, this point becomes a point of least action. From it, new least action paths coming from the past and going to the future are possible. It's as if the memory of the universe received a slight jolt, so that it forgot how it got that object to that particular place in space and time. Since the observation of the object now constitutes "fact," it becomes more reliable as a standpoint to predict the future. Thus, from the observed fact, a new least action path to the future is possible.

If we are "hung up" on the past, we will choose to see the future as we saw the past. If we alter our perception of the now, then our altered view will change the future! The question is how far can we go? How much can we change the future by altering our perception of the now? No one knows the answer. I believe that the idea of altering the "out there" reality by changing the "in here" observer is a very exciting and challenging prospect for research. Perhaps research into altered states of consciousness will show us the limits.

ANNOTATED BIBLIOGRAPHY

AND

ADDITIONAL READINGS

ANNOTATED BIBLIOGRAPHY

Asimov, Isaac. *The Genetic Code.* New York: New American Library, 1962.
———. *Life and Energy.* New York: Doubleday & Co., 1962.

Basic information on a popular level for those who want to critically evaluate the speculative idea of a biogravitational field that complements the DNA genetic code. For the layman.

Bass, L. "A Quantum-Mechanical Mind-Body Interaction." *Foundation of Physics 5* (1975): 159

Bass offers a quantum mechanical theory of consciousness with no added assumptions. Consciousness is choice acting at the atomic and molecular level of reality.

Belinfante, F. J. *A Survey of Hidden Variable Theories.* Elmsford, N.Y.: Pergamon Press, 1973.

  Advanced physics.

Benford, G.A., Book, D.L., and Newcomb, W.L. "The Tachyonic Antitelephone," *Physical Review, D.*V.2, 1970, p. 263.

Benford *et al* explain how detecting faster than light particles—that is tachyons—will lead to the building of a time machine—one that will receive messages from the future.

Bergman, P.G. *The Riddle of Gravitation.* New York: Charles Scribner's Sons, 1968.

A popular introduction to Einstein's general theory of relativity and blackhole physics. For the layman.

Bernstein, Jeremy. *Einstein.* New York: Viking Press, 1973.

An entertaining account of Einstein's ideas. For the layman.

Boeke, Kees. *Cosmic View.* New York: John Day Co., 1957.

Shows the different levels of organization of matter in space-time which are *perhaps* all connected by a cosmic bootstrap in the quantum foam. For the layman.

Bohm, David. "Quantum Theory as an Indication of a New Order in Physics." In *Quantum Theory and Beyond.* Edited by Ted Bastin. New York: Cambridge University Press, 1971.

On the linguistic structure of physics. Can be understood by the layman.

————. "A Suggested Interpretation of the Quantum Theory in Terms of 'Hidden' Variables." *Physical Review* 85 (1952): 166 and 180.

The major work on hidden variables in quantum theory. Presents the idea that quantum forces act without space-time limitations. Advanced physics.

Bonner, J.T. *The Scale of Nature.* New York: Pegasus, 1970.

Provides a perspective on the scientific world view. For the layman.

Borges, Jorge Luis. *Labyrinths.* New York: New Directions, 1964.

Contains a literary account of ideas of time and multiple universes that underlie much of the new physics. See for example *The Garden of Forking Paths* and compare to the Everett-Wheeler view of quantum theory.

de Broglie, Louis. "The Reinterpretation of Wave Mechanics." *Foundations of Physics I* (1970): 1–5.

A hidden variable approach to quantum theory. Advanced physics, can be partially understood by the layman.

Callen, E., and Shaperiv, D. "Theory of Social Imitation." *Physics Today* (July 1974): 23.

Shows deep universal patterns in nature. Illustrates Toben's speculation of a universal structure behind seemingly different phenomena on different levels. Advanced physics.

Capra, Fritjof. *The Tao of Physics.* New York: Bantam Books, 1977.

Shows how modern physics is closely related to Eastern philosophy. Highly recommended for the layman.

Carter, Brandon. "Global Structures of the Kerr Family of Gravitational Fields." *Physical Review.* 174 (1968): 1599.

———. "Complete Analytic Extension of the Symmetry Axis of Kerr's Solution of Einstein's Equations." *Physical Review.* 141 (1966): 1242.

This and other papers by Carter (1967–1970) contain the physical principles of time travel to the past. Some of these ideas are discussed in a popular way by Carl Sagan in his book, *The Cosmic Connection.* Carter's papers are advanced physics.

Caspar, D.L.D., and Klug, A. "Physical Principles in the Construction of Regular Viruses." *Cold Spring Harbor Symposia on Quantitative Biology* 27 (1962).

The patterns of nature. Can be understood by the layman with special interest.

Clifford, William Kingdon. *The Common Sense of the Exact Sciences.* New York: Dover Publications, Inc., 1955.

A nineteenth-century precursor to Einstein's geometrodynamics. Shows how variable space curvature can manifest as physical phenomena in an apparently flat space. A precognitive attempt to geometrize physics?

Culbertson, J.T. *The Minds of Robots.* Urbana: University of Illinois Press, 1963.

Tries to show how "mind" arises out of neural networks in space-time.

De Long, H. "Unsolved Problems in Arithmetic." *Scientific American* (March 1971): 50.

Popular discussion of Gödel's theorem, showing the duality between completeness and logical consistency of closed mathematical systems. This theorem may be relevant to the quantum duality of wave and particle and to our understanding of ESP.

D'Espagnat, Bernard. "The Quantum Theory and Reality." *Scientific American* (November 1979): p. 158.

A further recognition that human consciousness and physical reality cannot be separated. A clear explanation of Bell's theorem is presented.

DeWitt, B. and Graham, N., eds. *The Many-worlds Interpretation of Quantum Mechanics.* Princeton: Princeton University Press, 1973.

This contains Everett's remarkable thesis about the infinitely numbered universes interpretation of quantum mechanics. It also contains papers by other physicists describing their interpretations of Everett's interpretation.

Dirac, P. A. M. "The Lagrangian in Quantum Mechanics." Reprinted in *Quantum Electrodynamics,* edited by Julian Schwinger. New York: Dover Publications, Inc., 1958.

Duncan, Ronald and Weston-Smith, Miranda. *The Encyclopedia of Ignorance.* See W. Roxburgh, "The Cosmical Mystery," p. 37. Pergamon Press, 1977.

Professor Roxburgh offers us the idea of Paul Dirac—that the cosmological constants of nature are not constant after all. The many physical constants of nature can be grouped and rearranged into numerical values that are dimensionless numbers. Perhaps these numbers are not as arbitrary as they may seem.

See also: Feynman, R. P. "Space-Time Approach to Non-Relativistic Quantum Mechanics." Reprinted in *Quantum Electrodynamics,* edited by Julian Schwinger. New York: Dover Publications, Inc., 1958.

These books contain the basic physics leading to quantum electrodynamics and the new physics notion of multiple universes. For the advanced physicist.

Eccles, Sir John C. "The Physiology of Imagination." *Scientific American* (September 1958). Reprinted in *Altered States of Awareness,* edited by Timothy J. Teyler. San Francisco: Freeman, 1972.

A discussion of the basic physics of nerves. Can be understood by the layman. *See also:* Quarton, G. C. et al. *The Neurosciences.* New York: Rockefeller University Press, 1967.

Eddington, Sir Arthur. *The Nature of the Physical World.* Ann Arbor: University of Michigan Press, 1968.

————. *New Pathways in Science.* Ann Arbor: University of Michigan Press, 1959.

A highly original approach to physics with idealist tendencies. A precursor to the new physics that is developing in the 1970s among the counterculture physicists.

————. *The Philosophy of Physical Science.* Ann Arbor: University of Michigan Press, 1974.

Edmonds, James D., Jr. "Quaternion Quantum Theory: New Physics or Number Mysticism?" *American Journal of Physics* 42 (March 1974): 220.

Contains the Feynman, Dyson, and Einstein quotes used in commentary. Questions basic ideas about the nature of space-time. For physicists and adventurous laymen.

Eigen, Manfred. "Self-organization of Matter—The Evolution of Biological Macromolecules." *Naturwissenschaften* (February 1971).

Gives a chemical picture of self-organization complementary to the biogravitational meta-principle. Can be partially understood by the layman with background in biology and mathematics.

Einstein, Albert. *The Meaning of Relativity*. Princeton University Press, 1945.

See also: Wheeler, John A., et al. *Space-Time Physics*. San Francisco: Freeman, 1971.

Einstein's classic book can be partly understood by a reader with some background in physics. Einstein also wrote a little book titled *Relativity,* which can be understood by the layman. A knowledge of algebra and trigonometry is required for *Space-Time Physics.*

————, Lorentz, H. A., Weyl, H., and Minkowski, H. *The Principle of Relativity.* New York: Dover Publications, Inc., 1952.

A reprinting of classic papers in relativity theory.

Feldman, Laurence M. "Short Bibliography on Faster-Than-Light Particles (Tachyons)." *American Journal of Physics* 42 (March 1974).

Advanced physics.

Feynman, Richard P., Leighton, Robert B. and Sands, Matthew. *The Feynman Lectures on Physics,* Volumes I, II, and III. Reading, Mass.: Addison-Wesley Publishing Co., 1965.

These lectures are intended for physics students. I (FAW) found them extremely exhilarating and full of profound insights into physics. Readers may find them difficult.

Finkelstein, David. "The Space-Time Code." *Physical Review 5D* no. 12 (June 15, 1972): 2922.

An attempt to transcend continuum ideas of space-time. Highly speculative. Advanced physics. Contains idea of universe as a cosmic computer, attributed to R. P. Feynman. Perhaps a cosmic brain is more accurate? Hence an idealistic physics.

Fraser, Allan, and Frey, Allan H. "Electromagnetic Emission at Micron Wavelengths from Active Nerves." *Biophysical Journal* (June 1968): 731.

Physics of nerve action. Can be understood by the layman with a scientific background.

Gamow, George. *Biography of Physics*. New York: Harper & Row, 1961. *See also:* Gamow's *Mr. Tompkins in Paperback*, London: Cambridge University Press, 1965; *One, Two, Three . . . Infinity*, New York: Viking Press, 1961.

Very entertaining accounts of the great ideas of modern physics. Recommended for the layman.

Gardner, Martin. *The Ambidextrous Universe*. New York: New American Library, 1969.

A discussion of symmetry breakdown vital to the new physics. Recommended for the layman.

Gautreau, Ronald and Hoffman, Banesh. "The Schwarzchild radial coordinate as a measure of proper distance." *Physical Review D*, 17 (1978): 2552.

A clear and simple paper for scientists, high school science teachers and others who wish to gain a clear view of the subtlety of measurements near a black hole.

Glansdorff, P. and Prigogine, I. *Thermodynamic Theory of Structure, Stability and Fluctuations*. New York: John Wiley & Sons, 1971.

The role of nonlinear irreversible thermodynamics in the creation of living matter. An alternative to the biogravitational field approach?

Goldman, Stanford. "Mechanics of Individuality in Nature." *Foundations of Physics 1* (1971): 395; *3* (1973): 203.

Lends support to the concept of synchrosimilarity in nature. Can be understood by the layman.

Hawking, S.W., and Ellis, G. *The Large-Scale Structure of Space-Time*. Cambridge: Cambridge University Press, 1973.

The basic physics of black holes. Causality and time machines are discussed. Very advanced physics; difficult to understand.

Hawkins, David. *The Language of Nature*. San Francisco: W. H. Freeman, 1964.

A masterly view of basic ideas in physics, philosophy,

and consciousness. Highly recommended for the mature reader.

Heisenberg, Werner. *Physics and Beyond.* New York: Harper & Row, 1972.

———. *Physics and Philosophy.* New York: Harper & Row, 1966.

An account of the creation of quantum theory. Recommended for the layman.

James, William. *The Varieties of Religious Experience.* New York: New American Library, 1958.

A classic work relevant to the new synthesis of science with religion that will dominate the latter part of the twentieth century. Recommended for the layman.

Johnson, A. H. *Whitehead's Theory of Reality.* New York: Dover Publications, 1962.

A discussion of the idealist philosophy behind the new physics.

Josephson, Brian D. "The Discovery of Tunneling Supercurrents." *Science* 184 (May 3, 1974): 527.

See also: Anderson, Philip W. "How Josephson Discovered His Effect." *Physics Today* (November 1973): 23; Clarke, John. "Electronics with Superconducting Junctions." *Physics Today* (August 1971): 30; and Clarke, John. "Josephson Junctions Detectors." *Science* 184 (June 21, 1974): 1235.

These books discuss the discovery of a property of matter that may be vital for an understanding of life as a physical process. Recommended for the layman.

Klauder, J. R., ed. *Magic Without Magic.* San Francisco: W. H. Freeman, 1972.

A tribute to John A. Wheeler. Advanced physics.

Kaufmann, William J. III. *Relativity and Cosmology.* New York: Harper & Row, 1973.

A very good introduction to black hole physics and time machines. Recommended for the layman!

————. *The Cosmic Frontiers of General Relativity*. Boston: Little, Brown and Company, 1977.

In "Cosmic Frontiers" Kaufmann presents more about black holes including the diagrams of Kruskal, Penrose and others clearly explained. This is the best book I (FAW) have seen for the layperson describing without mathematics these wonderful constructions of human thought.

Kilmister, C. W. *General Theory of Relativity*. Elmsford, N.Y.: Pergamon Press, 1973.

A discussion of recent developments in general relativity. Relevant background material for understanding black holes, time machines, and PSI gravitronics operating *outside* the light cone. Advanced physics.

Kuhn, Thomas. *The Structure of Scientific Revolutions*. Chicago: University of Chicago Press, 1962.

On the nature of science and its value as a social activity. Can be understood by the layman with serious effort.

Leshan, Lawrence. *Toward a General Theory of the Paranormal*. New York: Parapsychology Foundation, Inc., 1969.

General discussion of the mystical viewpoint related to the thoughts of modern physics. Recommended for the layman.

Little, W. A. "Superconductivity at Room Temperature." *Scientific American* 212 (February 1965): 21. *See also:* Matthias, Bernd T. "The Search for High-Temperature Superconductors." *Physics Today* (August 1971): 23.

Discusses the discovery of a property of matter that may be vital for an understanding of life as a physical process.

Margenau, Henry. *Foundations of Physics*. (all issues).

A journal for the new physics. Layman reading level.

Marks, Robert W., ed. *Great Ideas in Modern Science*. New York: Bantam, 1967.

For the layman.

Motz, Lloyd. "Cosmology and the Structure of Elementary Particles." In *Advances in the Astronautical Sciences,* vol. 8. New York: Plenum Press, Inc., 1962.

The idea of strong finite-range gravity is introduced. Very advanced physics. Biogravitation, *if it exists,* must be of this type. Ordinary gravity is much too weak to organize living systems!

Newman, James R., ed. *World of Mathematics.* New York: Simon & Schuster, 1956. *See especially:* Vol. 1, pp. 548, 552, 563 (article by William Kingdon Clifford, "The Space Theory of Matter," etc.).

For the layman.

Ornstein, Robert. *The Nature of Human Consciousness.* San Francisco: W. H. Freeman, 1968.

A very useful collection of papers on consciousness, especially the papers by Blackburn and Tart. For the layman.

Penrose, Roger. "Structure of Space-Time." In *Battelle Rencontres 1967,* edited by J. A. Wheeler and C. De Witt. New York: Benjamin, 1967.

One of the classics of the new physics. Difficult to understand, but contains general philosophical passages of brilliant clarity that can be understood by the layman.

Prigogine, I., et al. "Thermodynamics of Evolution." *Physics Today* (November and December 1972). *See also: Thermodynamic Theory of Structure, Stability and Fluctuations.* New York: John Wiley, 1971.

An interesting but probably inadequate attempt to understand life as a physical process. Difficult reading, but may be understood by the layman.

Quarton, G. C., Melnechuk, T., and Schmitt, F. O. *The Neurosciences.* New York: Rockefeller University Press, 1967.

Comprehensive reference on the new biology.

Reichenbach, Hans. *Philosophic Foundations of Quantum Mechanics.* Berkeley: University of California Press, 1965.

For the mature scientific reader. Especially the idea of a non-Aristotelian logic to transcend the wave-particle quantum paradox.

Salam, Abdus. "Computation of Renormalization Constants." Preprint IC/71/3 from International Center of Theoretical Physics, Trieste, Italy, 1971.

See also: Isham, C. J., Salam Abdus, and Strathdee, J. "f-Dominance of Gravity." *Physical Review D* (February 15, 1971): 867–873; and Aichelburg, P. C. "Implications of Classical Two-Tensor Gravity." *Physical Review D* 8 (July 15, 1973): 377–384.

The idea of strong finite-range gravity is developed in a way independent of Motz's pioneering work. Extremely advanced physics. Considered speculative by conservative physicists. For an elementary discussion, see article by Dietrick Thomsen: *Science News* 99 (April 10, 1971): 249.

Sarfatti, Jack. "Implications of Meta-Physics for Psychoenergetic Systems." In *Psychoenergetic Systems,* vol. 1. London: Gordon and Breach Science Publishers, 1974.

For ambitious laymen and researchers in physics, philosophy, psychology, and parapsychology. A speculative hypothesis on the psychokinetic origin of quantum theory. A controversial document whose worth must be judged by experiments not yet performed. Views quantum jump as a scattering of a particle from a time-like path to a space-like path. Part of a *new* general relativity mechanics of the atom.

———. "The Primordial Proton." *Physics Today* (May 1974): 69. See misprint corrections in *Physics Today* (July 1974).

A speculation on how it all began. Advanced physics. *See also:* Sarfatti, Jack. "Gravitation, Strong Interactions and the Creation of the Universe." *Nature-Physical Science* (December 4, 1972).

———. "Quantum Mechanics as a Consequence of General Relativity." Int. Rep. IC/74/9. From the International Center of Theoretical Physics, Trieste, Italy, 1974.

————. "The Eightfold Way as a Consequence of the General Theory of Relativity." *Collective Phenomena* 1 (1974).

Salthouse, Andrew J. "Is Symmetry Breaking in SU(3) a Consequence of General Relativity?" Reprint UM HE 73–29 from The University of Michigan, Harrison Randall Laboratory, Ann Arbor, 1974.

Investigates some consequences of Dr. Sarfatti's research on the relation of quantum theory to general relativity. Fits Sarfatti's theory to some data on spectroscopy. Speculative attempt to link general relativity with quantum theory. Discusses quantum forces as disguised curvature effects. Advanced physics.

Schilpp, Paul Arthur. *Philosopher-Scientist Albert Einstein.* New York: Harper Bros., 1959.

For the mature science reader. Contains Einstein's autobiography.

Schrödinger, Erwin. *What Is Life?* New York: Doubleday & Co., 1956.

For the layman. Application of quantum theory to living matter.

Sciama, D. W. "Gravitational Waves and Mach's Principle." Preprint IC/73/94 from the International Center for Theoretical Physics, Trieste, Italy, 1974.

Shows how some phenomena need not be associated with wave field limited by space-time. Gives a new physics for phenomena exerting influences outside the light cone. The implication is that we must revise our ideas of information transfer. This is relevant to the Stanford Research Institute work on telepathy shown by Uri Geller and other psychics (*Nature,* October 18, 1974).

————. *The Unity of the Universe.* New York: Doubleday & Co., 1961.

For the layman.

Science News. "Physics Made Simple." 106 (July 1974): 20.

Experimental evidence that elementary particles are miniblack holes which grow larger when measured from close up. Recommended for the layman.

Shapiro, Sidney. "Josephson Currents in Superconducting Tunneling: The Effect of Microwaves and Other Observations." *Physical Review Letters* 11 (July 15, 1963): 80.

Advanced physics.

Stapp, H. P. "S-Matrix Interpretation of Quantum Theory." *Physical Review D* 3 (1971): 1303.

Shows the quantum interconnectiveness or "web" concept. Advanced physics, however the philosophical parts can be understood by the layman. The S-matrix "web" is another way of describing the labyrinth of worm holes in three-dimensional space. Simple ideas of distance are illusory—part of the Maya!

Steigman, Gary. "Antimatter in the Universe." Int. Rep. IC/73/110. From the International Center of Theoretical Physics, Trieste, Italy, 1973.

Argues that there is not much antimatter in this particular universe. Can be understood by the layman with some scientific bacground.

Sullivan, Walter. "A Hole in the Sky." *The New York Times Magazine* (July 21, 1974).

Discusses *big* black holes, which are related to but should not be confused with tiny (mini-) black holes. Highly recommended for the layman.

Tiller, William A. "Disease as a Biofeedback Device for the Transformation of Man." *Proceedings* of the A.R.E. Medical Symposium, Phoenix, Arizona, forthcoming.

An important step in the direction of a new synthesis of science and mysticism. Contains highly controversial, detailed material not generally accepted. Can be understood by the layman.

Walker, Evan Harris. "The Nature of Consciousness." *Mathematical Biosciences* 7 (1970): 138–178.

One of the few serious studies on the physics of consciousness. Most of this paper can be understood by the layman with a background in philosophy and psychology.

Watson, James D. *The Double Helix*. New York: Atheneum, 1968.

For the layman. Shows that scientists are not morally superior to most men. An intimate view of scientific creation.

Weinberg, Steven. "Unified Theories of Elementary-Particle Interaction." *Scientific American* (July 1974): 50.

A recent attempt to unify some theories in physics neglecting general relativity. Can be understood by the layman.

Wheeler, John A. *Geometrodynamics*. New York: Academic Press, 1962.

The "bible" of the new physics. Contains the concept that matter is entirely made out of curved three-dimensional space that is crisscrossed by worm holes . . . the quantum foam. For the physicist, but can be partially understood by the adventurous layman.

———. "Geons." *Physical Review* 97 (1955): 511.

Shows how gravity is self-organizing because of its nonlinearity. Advanced physics.

———, with Misner, C., and Thorne, K. S. *Gravitation*. San Francisco: Freeman, 1973.

A comprehensive discussion of Einstein's theory in the light of recent discoveries. Can be read and understood by those with a technical-scientific background or the layman with a knowledge of college-level calculus.

———. In *The Physicist's Conception of Nature*. Edited by J. Mehra. Amsterdam: Reidel Publications, 1974.

Shows that the laws of nature are not immutable. There *is* something new under the sun. Strips away the prejudices of many scientists who could not believe in "paranormal" phenomena on principle. Recommended for the enthusiastic layman. Contains *implicitly* the idea that laws of physics are partly determined by the state of consciousness of the participator—a psychokinetic view of quantum theory.

Wiener, Norbert. *Cybernetics.* New York: MIT Press and John Wiley & Sons, Inc., 1961.

On the role of feedback in living systems and in robots.

Wigner, Eugene. *Symmetries and Reflections.* Bloomington: Indiana University Press, 1967.

A deep, masterly commentary on the fundamentals of physics. Recommended for the layman. Contains ideas on the role of consciousness in quantum theory—a view rejected by most conventional physicists.

Wolf, Fred Alan. *Taking the Quantum Leap—The New Physics for Nonscientists.* San Francisco: Harper & Row, Publishers, 1981.

A nonmathematical and entertaining version of the most perplexing issues in physics. From the earliest models of the atom to the present quantum model, Wolf traces the history of quantum physics. The book, in its later chapters discusses the implications of quantum physics for ourselves and our relationship to the world. This is a good place for the general reader to begin an understanding of contemporary physics.

Wooldridge, Dean E. *The Machinery of the Brain.* New York: McGraw-Hill, 1963.

A basic discussion of neuroscience.

Young, Arthur M. "Consciousness and Cosmology." In *Consciousness and Reality,* edited by Charles Muses and Arthur M. Young. New York: Outerbridge and Lazard, 1972.

A comprehensive collection of speculative essays on the nature of consciousness and space-time. Can be partially understood by the layman.

ADDITIONAL BOOKS
FOR THE GENERAL READER

TOWARD ANOTHER CONSCIOUSNESS

Dean, Stanley. "Metapsychiatry: The Confluence of Psychiatry and Mysticism." *Fields Within Fields,* No. 11 (Spring 1974): 3–11.

A psychiatrist relates psychiatry and mysticism, and discusses the "ultraconscious" experience as a phenomenon is latent within all of us.

De Ropp, Robert S. *The Master Game.* New York: Delacorte, 1968.

The quest for a higher consciousness through meditation and knowledge without the need for drugs by a recognized authority in psychology and drug control.

Einhorn, Ira. *78-187880.* New York: Doubleday Anchor, 1974.

An exciting visual poetry statement on the dawn of the transformation of consciousness by one of the key figures in the world movement.

Suarès, Carlo. *Memoir on the Return of Reb Yhshwh, Called Jesus.* Paris: Laffont, 1975.

Heralding the coming transformation in consciousness, the interpretation of the universes, the crumbling of existing structures. The most important statement by a man who has spent his life in search of understanding through the energy code of the Qabala.

Van Over, Raymond. *Unfinished Man.* New York: World, 1972.

A comprehensive view of the unknown. A call for a change that may be necessary for survival.

White, John, ed. *The Highest State of Consciousness.* New York: Doubleday, 1972.

A collection of writings by experts in various scientific disciplines and others, attempting to describe high states of consciousness in their respective terminologies.

PARANORMAL PHENOMENA DESCRIBED

Academy of Parapsychology and Medicine. *Dimensions of Healing: A Symposium.* Los Altos, California: Academy of Parapsychology and Medicine, 1972.

Talks presented by some of the most important researchers in paranormal healing and consciousness research.

Hammond, Sally. *We Are All Healers.* New York: Harper & Row, 1973.

A comprehensive, professional report of conversations with some of the most respected healers in England and America.

Ostrander, Sheila, and Schroeder, Lynn. *Psychic Discoveries Behind the Iron Curtain.* New York: Bantam, 1971.

Reporters describe the history of psychic phenomena behind the Iron Curtain and current research into these phenomena. The book was a major force in opening up America's eyes to the excitement of other possibilities. General, nonscientific descriptions.

Puharich, Andrija. *Beyond Telepathy.* New York: Doubleday Anchor, 1973.

A thorough, objective study of the physiological and chemical commonalities shown by shamans, witch doctors, yogins, and others in altered states of consciousness; studies of physical environment; important experiments by the major pioneer in modern parapsychological research.

Tompkins, Peter, and Bird, Christopher. *The Secret Life of Plants*. New York: Avon, 1974.

The important experiments of recent years indicating awareness, emotion in plants.

Watson, Lyall. *Supernature*. New York: Bantam, 1974.

A biologist looks at life and cosmic forces, offering his theories for phenomena that are difficult to explain from the normal limited viewpoint.

ALTERNATE UNIVERSE VIEWS

Blofeld, John. *The Tantric Mysticism of Tibet*. New York: Dutton, 1970.

The universe view of Tantric yoga in Tibet. The concluding chapters describe links with alternate realities.

Floyd, Keith. "Of Time and Mind." *Fields Within Fields*, No. 10 (Winter 1973–1974): 47–57.

On the illusion of time and the nature of consciousness. Should open the mind of the reader to the nonobjectivity of "reality."

LeShan, Lawrence. *The Medium, The Mystic and The Physicist*. New York: Viking, 1974.

General discussion of the mystical viewpoint related to the thought of modern physics. A highly recommended book by a psychologist, one of the key researchers in parapsychology, who has worked with Eileen Garret and who has spent years studying and teaching psychic healing.

———. *Toward a General Theory of the Paranormal*. New York: Parapsychology Foundation, 1969.

Opens up the possibility of an alternate overview. A major document. See note above.

Pearce, Joseph. *The Crack in the Cosmic Egg*. New York: Pocket Books, 1973.

Discusses and emphasizes how all may be constructed by thought. How all things may be possible. How there may not be an objective reality.

THE ORDER IN NATURE

Johnson, Raynor. *The Imprisoned Splendor*. Wheaton, ' Illinois: Quest.

A physicist takes a grand view of the order of the universe and the potential within man.

Koestler, Arthur. *The Roots of Concidence*. New York: Random House, 1972.

A respected scientific writer discusses order and synchronicity in nature, using some of the latest ideas from the visionary scientists as foundations for understanding.

Purce, Jill. *The Mystic Spiral*. New York: Avon, 1974.
A major work on the importance of the spiral in nature, art, and mythology. Illustrated with beautiful photographs, this book is the forerunner of another more detailed study that is to be published in the near future.

PERSONAL EXPERIENCES OF OTHER REALITIES, RELATED BY SCIENTISTS

Castaneda, Carlos. *The Teachings of Don Juan*. New York: Pocket Books, 1974.
    ———. *A Separate Reality*. New York: Pocket Books, 1974.
    ———. *Journey to Ixtlan*. New York: Pocket Books, 1974.
    ———. *Tales of Power*. New York: Simon & Schuster, 1974.

In a fascinating series of books, an anthropologist describes his apprenticeship to a Yaqui Indian brujo. The universe view of the mystics is vividly particularized in a fantastic unfolding of experiences over the years, leading Castaneda to a personal acceptance of other realities.

Lilly, John. *The Center of the Cyclone*. New York: Bantam, 1973.

Lilly, a respected scientist who did the pioneering studies on dolphin intelligence, takes himself on a memorable exploration of his own inner space, connecting with experiences and realities that can be accepted and understood only within a new universe view.

Puharich, Andrija. *The Sacred Mushroom*. New York: Doubleday Anchor, 1974.

A pioneer in parapsychological research, Puharich describes his work with a young man who was able to link up with the knowledge of a high priest of ancient Egypt and to transmit that knowledge to this time location.

THE STRUCTURE OF CONSCIOUSNESS/ENERGY

Suarès, Carlo. *The Cipher of Genesis*. New York: Bantam, 1973.

———. *The Song of Songs*. Berkeley: Shambala, 1972.

A deciphering of the ancient writings of the original Hebrew-language Bible by the world authority on the energy code of the Cabala. The Bible actually describes the "now" process, the interplay of basic archetypal energies that manifest in the cosmos and in man. It is a textbook of what is happening now.

———. "The Code," "The Cipher of Genesis." *Christopher Books*, Tree II (Summer 1971).

An abstract of Suarès' major works. See note above.

BOB TOBEN

Has been an architect, artist, investor, researcher, and cartoonist.

FRED ALAN WOLF, Ph.D.

FRED ALAN WOLF received his undergraduate training in physics at the University of Illinois, Urbana (B.S., 1957) and completed his graduate training in applied physics (M.S., 1959) and theoretical physics (Ph.D., 1963) at UCLA. For many years a professor of physics at San Diego State University, he has also traveled and held visiting professorships at the Hahn-Meitner Institut (Berlin), the University of Paris, the Hebrew University of Jerusalem, and Birbeck College of the University of London. He has also held consulting positions with several industries and governments.

He is a computer consultant, teacher and the author of *Taking the Quantum Leap—The New Physics for Nonscientists.* He is presently devoting himself to the communication of the ideas of science to as wide an audience as possible.

NEW AGE CLASSICS
ENDURING BOOKS FOR OUR TIME AND BEYOND

☐ 25748 **ZEN AND THE ART OF MOTORCYCLE** $4.95
MAINTENANCE, Robert M. Pirsig

The fabulous journey of a man in search of himself . . .
"Profoundly important . . . intellectual entertainment of
the highest order." —New York Times

☐ 26382 **DANCING WU LI MASTERS: An Overview** $4.95
of the New Physics, Gary Zukov

"The Bible" for those who are curious about the mind-
expanding discoveries of advanced physics, but who have
no scientific background.

☐ 26299-8 **ENTROPY: A New World View,** Jeremy Rifkin $4.50
Tells us why our existing world view is crumbling and
what will replace it.
"An appropriate successor to . . . SILENT SPRING, THE
CLOSING CIRCLE and SMALL IS BEAUTIFUL."
—Minneapolis Tribune

☐ 34343 **THE MIND'S I: Fantasies and Reflections** $12.95
on Self and Soul, Douglas R. Hofstadter
and Daniel C. Dennett

A searching, probing book that delves deeply into the
domain of self and self-consciousness. Co-authored by
the winner of the Pulitzer Prize.
"Invigorating . . . a heavy set of tennis for the brain."
—Village Voice

☐ 34279 **METAMAGICAL THEMAS: Questing for the** $14.95
Essence of Mind and Pattern,
Douglas R. Hofstadter

The national bestseller by the Pulitzer Prize-winning
author of GODEL, ESCHER, BACH.

For your convenience, use this handy coupon for ordering: